THE
POLITICS
OF
DUPLICITY

The Politics Of Duplicity

Re-Visiting The Jaffna Talks

Anton Balasingham

Fairmax Publishing Ltd.

Fairmax Publishing Ltd.
212 Manor Way
Mitcham, CR4 1EL.
Surrey, England.

First Edition 2000

First published by Fairmax Publishing Ltd 2000
Copyright © Anton Balasingham 2000

A catalogue record of this book is
available from the British Library

ISBN: 1-903679-00-1

Printed at:
The Print
45C Crusoe Rd,
Mitcham, Surrey.
CR4 3LG.

Cover Design:
T. Kannan

All Rights Reserved No part of this publication may be reproduced, stored in a retrieval system, or transmitted in any form or by any means, electronic, mechanical, photocopying, recording or otherwise, without the prior permission of the publishers.

*This book is dedicated to
my loving wife
Adele Anne*

Contents

Introduction	*1*
Chandrika's Peace Initiative	*9*
A Low-key Goverment Team	*19*
Economic Blockade as Central Issue	*24*
The Joint Statement	*28*
Contradictions In Perceptions	*35*
Declaration of Cessation of Hostilities	*64*
The Issue Of Foreign Delegates	*67*
A Fragile Peace	*77*
LTTE Confers With Foreign Delegates	*85*
Chandrika Takes Hardline Position	*95*
Controversy Over French Intermediary	*104*
LTTE Issues Deadline	*113*
The Fourth Round of Talks	*129*
Chandrika Repeats The Promises	*135*
Reflections On Failure Of Talks	*145*

List of Illustrations

01 Chennai meeting: From left to right, Ossie Abeygunasekara, Chandrika Kumaratunga, Vijaya Kumaratunga, Lawrence Thilagar, B. Nadesan, Anton Balasingham.

02 Mr. Anton Balasingham (third right) and Mr. Tamilselvan (second right) and the ICRC delegate Ms. Mary Perkins (right), discuss the arrangements for talks with the government delegates at Subash Hotel, when they first arrived in Jaffna.

03 The Sri Lanka government delegation is escorted to the talks by LTTE cadres.

04 Mr. Tamilselvan, Head of LTTE delegation, welcomes Mr. Balapatabendi, Head of Sri Lanka government delegation at the LTTE political headquarters, Jaffna.

05 The LTTE and government delegation engage in discussions during the first round of talks. The LTTE flag and Mr. Pirabakaran's photograph occupy centre stage.

06 Government's negotiating team led by Mr. Balapatabendi, and the LTTE delegation led by Mr. Tamilselvan, at the LTTE's political headquarters in Jaffna.

07 The government delegation headed by Mr. Balapatabendi (right to left) Mr. Lionel Fernando, Mr. Gunaratna, and Mr. Asirwatham who participated in the first round of talks.

08 The LTTE delegation headed by Mr. Tamilselvan, (Second left.)

09 The LTTE team led by Mr. V. Pirabakaran, leader of the Tamil Tigers (middle), Mr. Anton Balasingham (right) and Mr. Tamilselvan (left) engaged in a discussion with the international monitoring committee.

10 Mr. V. Pirabakaran, leader of the LTTE, welcomes Mr. Audun Holm of Norway, a member of the international monitoring committee, at the LTTE's political head office in Jaffna. Mr. Anton Balasingham is in the background.

11 The international monitoring committee consisting of (Left to Right) Lt. Col. Paul Henry Hosting from Netherland, Major General Clive Milner from Canada, Johan Gabrielsen and Audun Holm of Norway in discussion with the LTTE.

12 Head of the LTTE negotiating team Mr. Tamilselvan (left) greets Brig. Peries, a member of the government's delegation.

13 The ICRC residential delegate in Jaffna, Ms. Mary Perkins (right) along with other delegates. The ICRC played a crucial role facilitating the Jaffna talks.

14 The Buddhist monks set fire to copies of Kumaratunga's constitutional proposal.

Introduction

When the peace talks between the government of Chandrika Kumaratunga and the Liberation Tigers of Tamil Eelam (LTTE) collapsed in April 1995, international governments unreservedly condemned the Tamil Tigers for sabotaging the peace effort. Before the LTTE could argue its case, the world had already passed judgement on the Tigers. Alienated and isolated from the world by lack of communication and media access, the Tigers could not present their side of the story. The Sri Lanka regime succeeded in winning the world onto its side by an effective global disinformation campaign.

On the very day the peace talks were suspended and armed hostilities resumed, Sri Lanka unleashed a major propaganda war with a blistering attack on the LTTE. The government alleged that the Tamil Tigers had broken the peace talks without reason or logic and resumed the war without warning. The speed with which the Sri Lanka government moved left us wondering if it had been eagerly anticipating this turn of events. The government rapidly mobilised and utilised all avenues and resources available to a modern state to convince the international community that the LTTE was the enemy of peace. The Sri Lankan Foreign Minister Mr. Lakshman Kadigarmar called the foreign media and the diplomatic community based in Colombo to conferences in a bid to intensify the propaganda war worldwide. Mr. Kadirgamar also embarked on a personal diplomatic mission to several capitals to convince the Western nations that the LTTE was the guilty party behind the failure of the peace talks.

The LTTE had justifiable reasons and compulsions to withdraw from the negotiating process. The government was not acting in good faith. It

1

failed to fulfil its pledges and promises. The talks were dragging on for more than six months without direction and progress. We did not stipulate any impossible conditions, but rather sought relief to the Tamil population suffering enormously under the economic blockade and other bans imposed by the government. The Kumaratunga regime was merciless and adopted an uncompromising attitude. We did not withdraw from the talks abruptly as the government construed. We gave adequate advance notice extending to a period of three weeks instead of 72 hours as required by the truce agreement. We urged the government to implement the pledges before the set deadline. But the government failed to take the warning seriously. In the end we were left with no other choice but to make that painful decision.

We knew that in the realm of peace negotiations the blame usually falls on the withdrawing party. But it was unavoidable. In our case we confronted a cleverly devised trap. It was a peace trap for a long-term war. The central aim behind the government's strategy was to gain national and international support for a massive war effort to invade the north. Such support could only be obtained on proven grounds that the Tigers were not amenable to a peaceful political resolution of the conflict. The government's hidden strategy became known only in the later months and years as the 'war for peace' scheme revealed its ugly face. But at that time, when the talks collapsed, the government scored a propaganda victory and won the support of the international community. The world may have been duped by Kadirgamar's cunning diplomacy but the government's intended program of marginalising the Liberation Tigers from the Tamil masses failed miserably. The Tamil people were well aware that the LTTE fought for their interests, firmly and resolutely, during the entire peace process persistently calling for urgent solution to the day to day problems faced by our people. And most importantly it was our people who knew that the government was lying when it claimed the economic blockade was lifted and all essential items were flowing to the North. Our people soon realised that the government was involved in an exercise of political duplicity and the talks would not succeed. The initial euphoria among the

Tamil masses turned into bitter disappointment when the talks reached a stage of impasse. And when the talks collapsed and hostilities resumed the Tamil people were neither surprised nor dismayed.

A critical examination of the Jaffna peace talks is relevant today in the current political scenario as initiatives are mooted by the international community to revive the peace talks between the Sri Lanka government and the Liberation Tigers. A reappraisal of the Jaffna talks will also help to understand the mood and thinking of the Tamil Tigers in relation to political negotiations. The deep distrust shown by the LTTE towards the Kumaratunga government and its disinclination to re-enter into a peace dialogue has its roots in the disenchantment experienced by the LTTE leadership during the Jaffna talks. Furthermore, the Tigers continue to insist on the removal of oppressive conditions and normalisation of civilian life in the Tamil homeland as essential pre-requisites for peace talks - the very same themes advanced by our movement during the negotiations in Jaffna. Therefore, a re-examination of the Jaffna peace talks from the Tamil perspective, elucidating the problematic that underlie the failure of the negotiations is significant and relevant to comprehend the position of the LTTE on the question of peace and peaceful settlement of the conflict.

Adopting a peculiar modality hitherto unknown in the discourse of conflict resolution, the Jaffna peace talks were held on two levels. On the one level, there were direct negotiations between the accredited representatives of the Sri Lanka government and the Liberation Tigers. On the other level there was indirect dialogue between the leadership of the government and the LTTE in the form of exchange of letters. Both levels of talks lasted for a period of six months. In total there were four rounds of direct talks between the nominated delegates with each session lasting only for a day or two, allowing limited time to discuss a wide spectrum of issues. Since the government was represented by a low-key team without any authority to make decisions, the direct engagement produced no positive results and the correspondence between the leaderships became significant and determinant. As the Head of the Sri Lanka State,

Chandrika Kumaratunga corresponded with the LTTE leader Mr. Velupillai Pirabakaran. In the capacity of the Deputy Defence Minister Col. Ratwatte also exchanged a few letters with the LTTE leader particularly on the matters of security and cessation of hostilities. There were also letters of exchange between Mr. Balapatabendi, the head of the Sri Lanka delegation, and Mr. Tamilselvan, who led the LTTE negotiating team. In this study, we present the entire correspondence between the government of Kumaratunga and the Liberation Tigers in chronological order of narration with the analysis of the developments of the objective conditions. The correspondence was facilitated by the good offices of the International Committee of the Red Cross (ICRC).

The letters of exchange are important for any critical examination of Jaffna peace talks since the leadership of the parties in conflict articulated their respective positions through written correspondence. By close scrutiny of the correspondence one could find feelings of optimism and expectations in both circles during the early stages of the peace talks. But those positive sentiments soon died down to be replaced by a sense of bitterness and acrimony as problems cropped up in the later stages of the negotiations. Readers will find the letters polemical, contentious, argumentative, as both parties contested each others position and rationalised and legitimised their own. This polemic made some correspondence repetitive where both the parties reiterated and reasserted their mutual stands. We felt that the tone and contents of some of the letters written by Chandrika and Ratwatte were accusatory and hostile. They were skillfully constructed propaganda pieces written with an intention of releasing to the public at a later stage to shift the blame on to the LTTE if the talks failed. The government did release some selected correspondence soon after the talks collapsed. In this study we have released all correspondence with commentaries to explain the developing objective situation so that the reader can grasp the complexities of the problem. From the outset the LTTE proposed that the talks should proceed stage by stage. The early stages of the talks, the Tigers insisted, should focus on restoring conditions of peace and normalcy in the Tamil homeland. In this context the Tigers called for the removal of all oppressive blockades, bans and restrictions that seriously affected the social and economic life of our people and caused them enormous suffering. We wanted a stable condition of peace effected by a permanent cease-fire and normalisation of civilian life before embarking on a political dialogue to resolve the ethnic conflict. We felt that if Kumaratunga's government genuinely sought peace and ethnic reconciliation, it should, first of all, remove the repressive conditions imposed on our people and alleviate their long standing suffering.

Though the government initially agreed to the LTTE's agenda, it changed its position in due course when it encountered opposition from the military establishment for relaxing the blockades and bans. To circumvent the issue the government proposed discussing the political problems underlying the ethnic conflict first. But the LTTE continued to insist that the urgent existential problems faced by the people should be addressed and resolved prior to political negotiations. This conflictual position led to bitter debate in the correspondence, in which both parties accused each other of bad faith. Finally, the government adopted a hard line position arguing that blockades and bans imposed on the Tamils were necessary measures of national security that could not be compromised. The issue continued unresolved until the last stages, compelling the Tigers to issue a deadline for the discontinuation of talks.

From the very beginning of the talks, until the last phases, the government made occasional claims that it had lifted several essential items from the economic blockade but none of these items reached the people. The military personnel stationed at the border posts of Vavuniya ensured that lifted items did not reach the Tamil people. The government failed to take any action though the LTTE, as well as the public, complained and protested several times. There was collusion between the government and the military in maintaining the economic blockade. We realised later that the government was playing a deceitful game of propaganda to appease the international community as if it had been fair and kind to the Tamil people. But in reality the government was determined to perpetuate the conditions of oppression against the Tamils with ultimate military designs that became apparent after the talks collapsed.

The other crucial issue that led to the breakdown of talks was the ineffectual, loosely worked out truce that led to various incidents of cease-fire violations particularly in the East. The LTTE wanted a permanent, stable cease-fire with international supervision. But the government was not favorable to that proposition. Instead, it proposed a temporary unbinding cessation of hostilities without proper modalities and mechanisms of supervision. It also adopted delaying tactics in the formation of monitoring committees chaired by international experts. This disinclination to establish a stable cease-fire indicated to us that the government was not genuine in the pursuit of peace.

The matter that gave serious concern to the LTTE leadership was the systematic build up of the Sri Lankan military machine during the period of peace negotiations. Sri Lanka took measures to expand and modernise the armed forces in violation of the principles of the truce agreement that demanded the parties in conflict to maintain military status quo. We had evidence to believe that the Kumaratunga government was operating on a hidden agenda of a grand military plan to invade the Jaffna peninsula and the Northern mainland which were under our control. The peace talks provided time and space for the Kumaratunga government to organise a massive military buildup. This clandestine military project became transparent when the talks failed. The massive procurement of modern weapon systems, large scale movement of troops from the East to the Palaly military complex in Jaffna and other war preparations which took place soon after the ill-fated talks, confirmed our apprehensions of an imminent military invasion of Jaffna. Thus, Kumaratunga's peace initiative transformed into a massive war effort under the slogan of 'War For Peace' which still continues after five years of cataclysmic destruction in life and property.

In providing a critical analysis of the Jaffna peace talks we argue that this peace making enterprise was undertaken in bad faith. There was no genuine will or determination on the part of the Sri Lanka government to win the goodwill, trust and confidence of the Tamil people. This could have been easily obtained by alleviating some of the hardships and suffering of the Tamil people. The state has legal and moral obligations to promote the welfare of its citizens, if it considers the Tamil people its citizens. But the government failed to act with responsibility, fairness and justice. The peace enterprise did not dispel the historical distrust and hatred between the protagonists in conflict but rather helped to deepen the hostility and drive them to adopt intractable and entrenched positions. This study will also help to understand the prevailing contradictions between the parties and the reasons for the current impasse in the peace efforts.

Chandrika's Peace Initiative

My first and only encounter with Chandrika Kumaratunga was in Chennai (formally Madras) during the early part of 1986 when our political offices and military training bases were functioning in Tamil Nadu, India. The lady paid a visit to our political headquarters at Indira Nagar, Adiyar accompanied by her husband Vijaya Kumaratunga and Ossie Abeygunasekara of the Sri Lankan Mahajana Party. Vijaya Kumaratunga was a radical politician with a sympathetic understanding of the freedom struggle of the Liberation Tigers who had visited Jaffna and met Tiger leaders to exchange prisoners of war.

At the time of our encounter, Chandrika was not seriously involved in Sri Lankan politics but showed intense curiosity over the political aims and objectives of the LTTE. For nearly an hour, I gave a thorough theoretical exposition of the Tigers political project arguing our case for political independence and statehood based on the right to self-determination of the Tamil people. While her husband listened politely with patience Chandrika was argumentative. Presenting a pluralistic model of Sri Lanka's social formation, comprising of different ethnic groupings, she rejected the conception of Tamil nation and Tamil homeland. Chandrika's thesis, in essence, was that the Tamil problem was a minority issue, not a nationality question and that the Tamils were not entitled to the right to self-determination and statehood. I tried to convince her that the Tamil people inhabiting the Northeastern region of Sri Lanka constituted a national formation as they have a distinct language, culture, history, a contiguous territory, a unique economic life and a feeling of oneness as a distinct people. These are the objective and subjective elements universally regarded as essential components that constitute a nation or a people. Furthermore, I pointed out that the Northeast has been the historical habitation of the Tamils for centuries and therefore it was their homeland. The Tamils had their own kingdom and enjoyed statehood until western colonism deprived them of their sovereignty over their natural and historical territory. As a nation of people living in their own homeland the Tamils were entitled to the right to self-determination, I said. Explaining further, I stated that self-determination was a right of a people to freely determine their political status and destiny. As legitimate bearers of the right to self-determination, our people chose to invoke this right in the 1977 general elections calling for the formation of the independent Tamil state. Chandrika objected by arguing that the Tamils could not exercise the right to secede within a unitary state. I argued that the Tamils could exercise the right to choose their political status in a specific historical condition when they were politically alienated and not represented in government and when the State became an alien force of domination, and racist repression assumed intolerable proportions. The lady was obstinate and single-minded. She operated with a different mind-set, from a different ideological universe. I could notice an inherent resistance in her to tolerate any alternative themes other than her well entrenched pluralist conception of Sri Lankan society in which all ethnic minorities have to adjust and associate with the majority. Rejecting my arguments underlying the Tamil national question she retorted, 'Why can't the LTTE persuade the Tamils to live in peace and harmony with the Sinhalese instead of fighting for the division of the country'. I was really annoyed.

Having observed my frustration, Mr. Kumaratunga intervened to enlighten his wife. 'The Tamil people are fighting for an independent state because they have been oppressed and discriminated against by successive Sri Lankan governments' he said. At this point I taunted

Chandrika by saying that her parents were the main architects of Sinhalese chauvinistic oppression that compelled the Tamils to seek secession. For a moment she was cornered and embarrassed, but she managed to compose herself and remarked, 'therefore the solution lies in the removal of the conditions of oppression rather that fighting for secession'. Thereafter the discussion centred on the eradication of the conditions of oppression. I argued that the main Sinhala political parties, the UNP and the SLFP, were essentially chauvinistic and therefore incapable of transformation. Agreeing with my contention, Mr. Kumaratunga said that a radically new political movement with an enlightened policy should emerge to resolve the problems of the Tamil people. At the end of the dialogue, the lady proclaimed she would enter politics in Sri Lanka one day and that if she comes to power she would bring peace and ethnic harmony to the island by removing the conditions of oppression imposed on the Tamils.

Eight years after the meeting with the Tamil Tigers in Tamil Nadu, Chandrika assumed political power as the head of a new Sri Lanka government. But how far did she fulfil her promise to remove the conditions of oppression imposed on our people when she was provided with an ideal opportunity to do so in 1994? This study will attempt to demonstrate that she failed to fulfil her promise. Furthermore, her term of office turned out to be the most oppressive period in Sri Lankan political history.

The central theme of Chandrika's electoral campaign was peace. She pledged that if she was elected to power, she would enter into a peace dialogue with the Tamil Tigers and bring an end to the war. At a pre-election meeting at Nugegoda in a suburb of Colombo, Chandrika proclaimed that she would concede the rights of the Tamils and honourably withdraw the armed forces from the Northeast. Projecting herself as a goddess of peace and non-violence, Chandrika extended the hand of friendship to the LTTE, pleading for peace and promising ethnic reconciliation. To an island tormented by war and violence for nearly two decades, her message of peace was powerful and enticing. The People's Alliance swept to victory at the general elections. Chandrika Kumaratunga was sworn in as the Prime Minister on the 19th of August 1994.

For nearly 17 years, the United National Party ruled the island with tyranny and oppression. In those turbulent years, characterised by armed conflict in the Northeast and insurrection and unrest in the South, it was the Tamil nation that suffered enormously. Ruling the Tamil nation with draconian emergency laws, the UNP regime intensified military brutality, subjecting the Tamil civilian masses to the extremes of state terror and persecution. Furthermore, the UNP rulers imposed economic blockades on the Tamil nation, banning all essential items crucial for the sustenance of life. These repressive measures created an acute shortage of food and medicine. The ban on fuel (petrol, diesel and kerosene) paralysed industry and transport. The embargo on fertilisers crippled agriculture. The ban on fishing reduced the Tamil fishing community to nightmarish conditions of poverty. Telecommunication links to the North were severed. Electricity generating plants were bombed, plunging the Jaffna peninsula into darkness of a primitive age. Furthermore the freedom of mobility of our people was curtailed by restrictions on travel. The United National Party administration imposed these oppressive measures as necessary conditions to facilitate the state's military campaign in the Tamil homeland and to deny the Tamil resistance movement essential supplies, callously disregarding the fact that such measures profoundly affected the social and economic life of the entire population.

It was against this background that Chandrika promised peace and salvation to our people and offered unconditional talks to the Tigers. Within a fortnight of assuming State power, she relaxed the economic embargo on certain items as a demonstration of her goodwill. The LTTE leadership was compelled to respond to Chandrika's humanitarian gesture. From the outset, Mr Pirabakaran, the leader of the LTTE, was sceptical of Chandrika's gesture. He felt it was a political gimmick to win the support of the Tamils and Sinhalese for the forth-coming presidential elections. I advised him to respond to her positively. "She is a new leader emerging on the Sri Lankan political horizon articulating progressive politics. It would be politically prudent on our part to initiate a dialogue with her government to find out whether or not she is genuine in resolving the problems of the Tamils," I told Mr. Pirabakaran. He agreed.

On the 2nd of September, Mr. Pirabakaran issued a press statement welcoming Chandrika's gesture of goodwill. In the statement, he announced his decision to release ten police detainees as 'a reciprocal gesture of goodwill'. He urged Chandrika to lift the economic blockade totally, to create conditions of normalcy in the Tamil homeland. He also suggested a permanent cease-fire and unconditional talks. A copy of the statement was sent to Chandrika through the good offices of the International Committee of the Red Cross. Following is the text of the signed statement by Mr. Pirabakaran:

LTTE Headquarters
Jaffna
2.9.1994

We sincerely welcome the decision made by the new Government of Mrs. Chandrika Kumaratunga to partially lift the economic embargo imposed on our people by the previous regime. We consider this step a constructive measure to create a congenial atmosphere of peace and goodwill.

As a positive response to the Government's conciliatory gesture we have decided to release ten (10) police detainees who are held in our custody as prisoners of war. We earnestly believe that our decision to release a section of the detainees will be viewed as a reciprocal gesture of goodwill and understanding.

We wish to point out that the economic embargo imposed on our people by the previous regime was an act of grave injustice and inhumanity. For the last four years our people have been subjected to enormous suffering without the essentials of daily existence. In this context, the positive step taken by the new Government to relax the embargo will be very much appreciated by our people. We hope that the Government will soon lift the economic embargo totally, paving the way for the restoration of normalcy in Tamil areas. The new Government could claim to have done justice only when the essential commodities that are freely available to the Sinhala people are made available to our people.

We wish to reiterate that we are prepared for cease-fire and unconditional talks. We are willing to co-operate with the new Government in all efforts to create congenial conditions of peace and normalcy, which are conducive for the conduction of peace negotiations.

(V.Pirabakaran)
Leader
Liberation Tigers of Tamil Eelam

A week later, Chandrika responded. A brief message was transmitted to Mr. Pirabakaran through the ICRC on the 9th September 1994 welcoming our decision to participate in the peace talks. She also requested us to nominate accredited representatives to begin discussions with her nominees. In the letter, she promised to restore electricity 'as far as possible' and repair the highway and parts of the irrigation schemes. We publish here below the full text of the message.

9th September 1994

Mr. V. Pirabakaran
Leader
Liberation Tigers of Tamil Eelam
LTTE Headquarters
Jaffna

Dear Mr. Pirabakaran,

We are happy to note that the LTTE has welcomed our gesture of goodwill towards the people of Jaffna and North in lifting the embargo imposed by the previous Government. We appreciate the decision taken by the LTTE to release ten police detainees who were held in the LTTE custody for several years and consider this gesture as one of goodwill and a demonstration of your positive intentions to negotiate the solutions to the problems of North and East.

We have noted with much interest your statement that you are prepared for peace talks. We would like to discuss this matter in greater detail. We suggest that you nominate representatives to begin discussions with my nominees.`

We would like to ensure that items for which the embargo was lifted reach the people of Jaffna without any delay. In this matter, we find difficulty as we have only Point Pedro to which we could transfer the goods directly. We would like to work out the ways and means we could get these goods without delay to the people of Jaffna.

Our Government has also decided to restore, as far as possible, electricity, repair the major highways and part of the irrigation schemes, as further normalisation of civil life.

We welcome your offer of co-operation in our Government's efforts towards peace and restoring normalcy in the North and East.

We therefore expect you to extend all co-operations to our technical officers who would be handling the repair works in the above stated development projects.

I suppose that the discussions I have suggested between your nominee and mine could also work out the modalities of this exercise.

Thanking you.
Yours Sincerely,

Chandrika Bandaranaike Kumaratunga
Prime Minister

Chandrika did not comment on Mr Pirabakaran's request for the total removal of the economic embargo nor did she make any reference to our call for a cease-fire. Furthermorem, she asked us to nominate our representatives without indicating to us the status or rank of the Government nominees. Nevertheless, we decided to appoint four of our senior cadres including Mr. Karikalan, Deputy Head of Political Section, as our accredited representatives. We decided to raise the issue of the economic embargo and other restrictions as urgent and immediate problems during preliminary discussions with the Government representatives. Mr. Pirabakaran was unhappy over the unwillingness on the part of the government to effect a cessation of hostilities before the commencement of the peace talks. We were anxious that the ongoing armed confrontations might cause a serious incident that might hamper the peace process.

In his letter to Chandrika Kumaratunga dated 12.9.1994, Mr. Pirabakaran nominated the LTTE's representatives and expressed regret that the Government had ignored his suggestion for a cease-fire. He emphasised that cessation of armed hostilities was essential for an environment of peace and goodwill and for the normalisation of civilian life. The following is the text of the letter:

LTTE Headquarters
Jaffna
12.9.1994

Hon. Chandrika Bandaranaike Kumaratunga
Prime Minister
Sri Lanka
Dear Prime Minister,

We are pleased to receive your letter dated 9th September 1994. We are glad to note that you have welcomed our gesture of goodwill by releasing ten detainees in our custody.

We appreciate your sincere concern that the goods for which the economic embargo was lifted should reach the people of Jaffna without delay. We share a mutual concern in this issue and would be glad to assist you in your endeavour to find ways and means to resolve this urgent problem.

We welcome the decision of your government to restore electricity, repair highways and renovate irrigation schemes. We wish to assure you that the LTTE will extend its fullest co-operation and assistance to the Government's technical officers who would be involved in the renovation work.

We appreciate your favourable response to our call for peace talks. You have suggested that we nominate our representatives to begin preliminary discussions. We therefore, nominate the following persons as our accredited representatives to conduct initial talks. Your nominees could also discuss with our representatives the modalities involved in the renovation work of the proposed development projects. Our nominees are:

1. *Mr. K. Karikalan*
   Deputy Head of Political Section

2. *Mr. S. Elamparuthy*
   Political Organiser
   Jaffna District

3. *Mr. A. Ravi*
   Head of Department of Economic
   Research and Development

4. *Mr. S. Dominique*
   Head of Department of Public
   Administration

Furthermore, we note with regret that no reference is made in your letter to our suggestion for cease-fire. You will appreciate that cessation of hostilities is a crucial element in the process of building up an atmosphere of peace, goodwill and normalisation of civilian life. I hope that you will consider this matter in earnest.

Thanking you.
Yours Sincerely.

(V.Pirabakaran)
Leader
Liberation Tigers of Tamil Eelam

For more than a week, we did not get any response from Chandrika. In the meantime land and sea battles raged between the LTTE fighters and the Sri Lankan armed forces. Sri Lankan combat aircraft continued their regular bombing sorties, causing civilian casualties. A serious incident occurred on the night of 19th September 1994 in a ferocious sea battle on the Mannar seas. In the confrontation a Sri Lankan frigate called 'Sargarawardane' was attacked and sunk by the Sea Tigers in the Gulf of Mannar. Twenty-four sailors were killed in the incident. The captain of the warship and another naval officer were rescued and taken as prisoners of war. We thought that this incident might upset the new government. But the statement made by a government minister that incidents of armed conflict would not impede the peace process allayed our apprehension.

On the 21st of September, just two days after the incident, Mr Pirabakaran received a brief message from Chandrika nominating the government representatives for discussions. The text of the message was the following:

21st September 1994

Mr. V. Prabhakaran
Leader
Liberation Tigers of Tamil Eelam
LTTE Headquarters
JAFFNA
Dear Mr. Pirabakaran,

I thank you for your letter date 12th September 1994 nominating your four representatives for discussion with us. I give below the names of our Government's representatives: -

1. Mr. K. Balapatabendi -
   Secretary to the Prime Minister, Attorney- at- Law

2. Mr. Lionel Fernando -
   Secretary, Ministry of Information, Tourism Aviation

*3. Mr. R. Asirwatham -
Chairman, Bank of Ceylon and
Senior Partner for, Rhodes & Thornton*

*4. Mr. N.L. Gooneratne -
Chairman, Design Consortium Ltd. (Architect)*

This team could visit Jaffna for the initial discussion for 02 days, any time between the 3rd-6th October or 12th -15th October 1994.

Could you kindly inform us, which days would suit you and also the venue you suggest and other related details?

*Thanking you.
Yours Sincerely*

*Chandrika Bandaranaike Kumaratunga
Prime Minister*

A Low-key Goverment Team

We were deeply disappointed when we received the list of government nominees for talks. The team consisted of a lawyer, a civil servant, a bank manager and an architect. We were perplexed as to why senior politicians with wider knowledge of the Tamil ethnic conflict were not included in the government's negotiating team. The nominees seemed to be personal emissaries or confidantes of Chandrika who lacked professional experience in peace negotiations nor did they possess any political authority to make decisions. None of them had any knowledge of the history either of the Liberation Tigers or of the armed liberation struggle. At a later stage in the course of the dialogue, we realized the government representatives were not men of innovative ideas or experts in conflict resolution, but simply bearers of messages who carried information to a supreme authority in Colombo.

Having scrutinized the list of nominees, Mr. Pirabakaran told me that Chandrika was neither serious nor earnest in seeking a peace dialogue with the Tamil Tigers. The LTTE leader felt that the Kumaratunga government was treating the Tamil Tigers as an illegal rebel movement functioning outside the framework of constitutional politics, not as a liberation organisation representing the Tamil nation. There would be no parity between the parties in conflict at the negotiating table. By nominating a low key team without political knowledge or power, we felt the government was deliberately devaluing the significance of the direct negotiations. Though we were dismayed, we decided to participate in the peace talks, hoping that Chandrika would induct senior politicians in the later stages of the dialogues as the talks progressed.

The following are letters of exchange between Mr. Pirabakaran and Chandrika Kumaratunga dealing with the dates, venues and other related matters of the peace talks. Included here is a letter dated on the 11th of October 1994 written to Mr. Pirabakaran by the Secretary to the Prime Minister Mr. K. Balapatabendi, proposing an agenda for the discussions.

LTTE Headquarters
Jaffna
23.9.1994

Hon. Chandrika Bandaranaike Kumaratunga
Prime Minister
Sri Lanka
Dear Prime Minister,

We are pleased to receive your letter dated 21st September 1994 in which you have nominated your Government's representatives for preliminary talks.

We are glad to inform you that your nominees are welcome in Jaffna any time between 12th - 15th October 1994. Nevertheless, the 13th - 14th October 1994 will be the most convenient dates for us.

Chennai meeting: From left to right, Ossie Abeygunasekara, Chandrika Kumaratunga, Vijaya Kumaratunga, Lawrence Thilagar, B. Nadesan, Anton Balasingham.

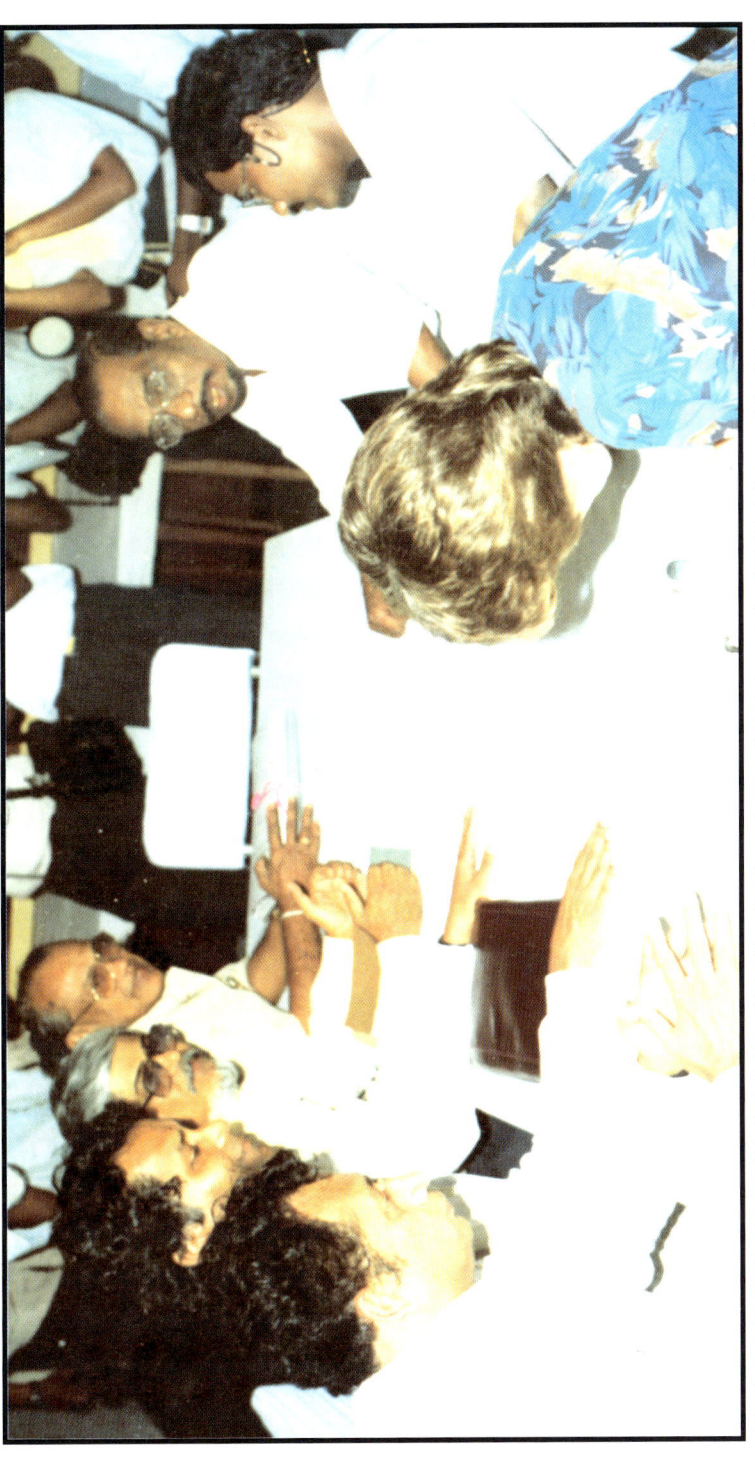

Mr. Anton Balasingham (third right) and Mr. Tamilselvan (second right) and the ICRC delegate Ms. Mary Perkins (right), discuss the arrangements for talks with the government delegates at Subash Hotel, when they first arrived in Jaffna.

The Sri Lanka government delegation is escorted to the talks by LTTE cadres.

Mr. Tamilselvan, Head of LTTE delegation, welcomes Mr. Balapatabendi, Head of Sri Lanka government delegation at the LTTE political headquarters, Jaffna.

The LTTE and government delegation engage in discussions during the first round of talks. The LTTE flag and Mr. Pirabakaran's photograph occupy centre stage.

Government's negotiating team led by Mr. Balapatabendi, and the LTTE delegation led by Mr. Tamilselvan, at the LTTE's political headquarters in Jaffna.

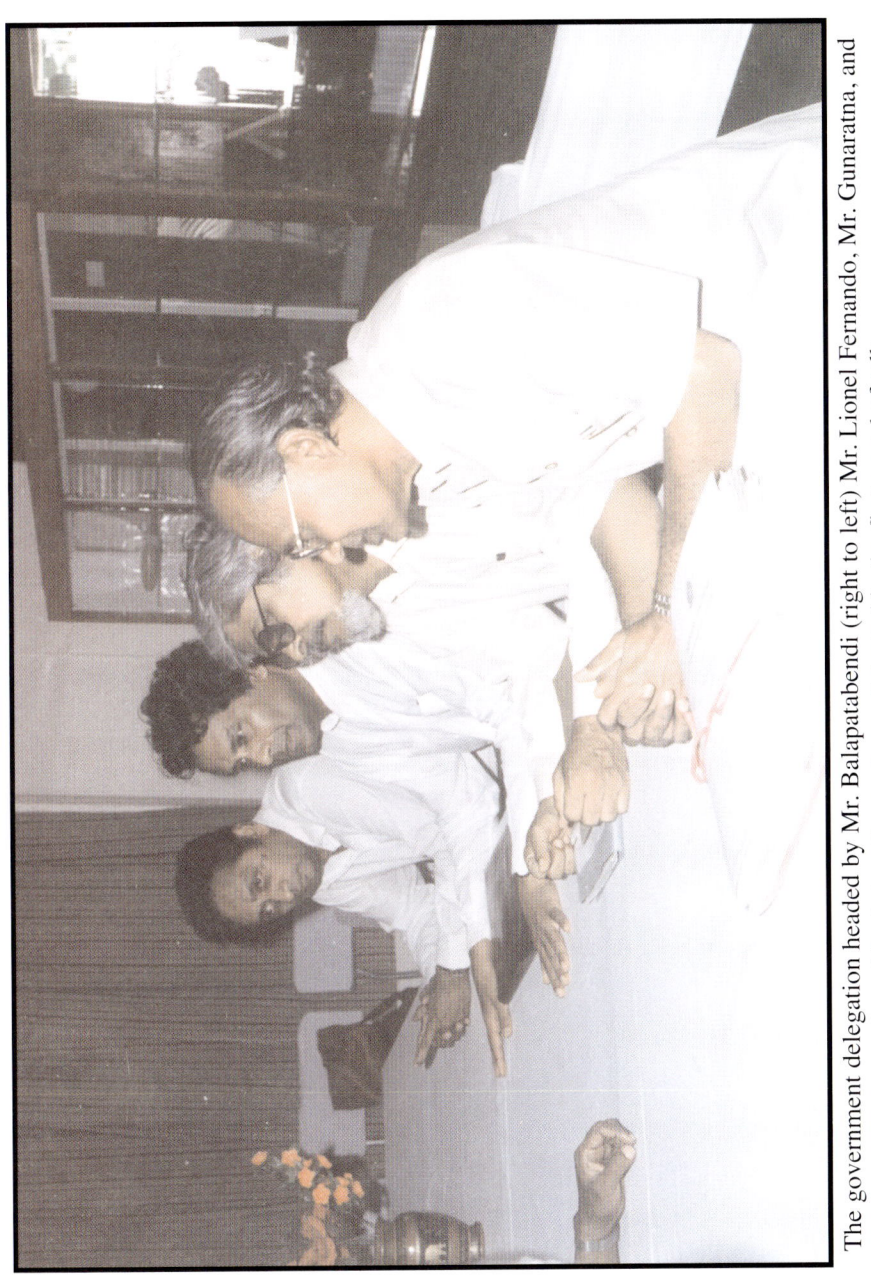

The government delegation headed by Mr. Balapatabendi (right to left) Mr. Lionel Fernando, Mr. Gunaratna, and Mr. Asirwatham who participated in the first round of talks.

The LTTE delegation headed by Mr. Tamilselvan, (Second left.)

We wish to assure you that the LTTE will assume full responsibility for the safety and security of your representatives during their stay in Jaffna. The details of the venue and other related matters will be communicated to you through the good offices of the ICRC in Jaffna.

Thanking you.
Yours Sincerely.

(V.Pirabakaran)
Leader
Liberation Tigers of Tamil Eelam

6th October 1994

Mr. V. Pirabakaran
Leader
Liberation Tigers of Tamil Eelam
LTTE Headquarters
JAFFNA
Dear Mr. Pirabakaran,

I thank you for your letter dated 23rd September 1994. All arrangements have been made for the visit of our delegation to Jaffna on 13th and 14th October 1994.

They will arrive by helicopter to the Palaly base and stay the night there. We shall be grateful if you could arrange to take them to and from Palaly Camp to the place of discussions with you. The flight details will be conveyed to you on the 10th October.

They will bring our proposed agenda for discussions, which will be sent to you by 10th October. We suppose that you will have your agenda prepared before hand.

It would be appreciated if our delegation could visit Jaffna and meet some persons. We will convey details also on 10th October.

Would you mind if a photographer accompanies our delegation, or would you provide one?
With kind regards.
Yours Sincerely

Chandrika Bandaranaike Kumaratunga
Prime Minister

LTTE Headquarters
Jaffna
8th October 1994

Hon. Chandrika Bandaranaike Kumaratunga
Prime Minister
Sri Lanka
Dear Prime Minister,

I am pleased to receive your letter dated 6th October 1994 confirming the visit of your delegation to Jaffna on the 13th and 14th October 1994.

We have made arrangements to receive your delegates in Jaffna, the details of which have already been communicated to you through the good offices of the ICRC.

We have suggested that your delegation could arrive in Jaffna by helicopter on the morning of the 13th October. We proposed that the open area at the front of the Jaffna University (between the Hindu temple and Sir P. Ramanathan Road) could be used as a suitable landing place for the helicopter. We assume responsibility for the safety of the helicopter and crew during this exercise.

If there are any difficulties in arranging this mode of air transport which is convenient and time saving, we suggest that the assistance of the ICRC could be sought to bring the delegation by boat from KKS to Point Pedro where they will be received by the LTTE delegates.

Subash Hotel, which is situated within the security zone of the Jaffna Hospital, will be the place of accommodation for the visiting delegates. The delegates will be escorted to our political office at Chundukuli, which will be the venue for talks. As I have stated in my letter dated 23.9.1994, the LTTE will provide full security to the visiting delegates. Arrangements can be made for your delegates to meet any persons at their place of accommodation. A photographer accompanying the delegates will be welcome.

Please confirm transport arrangements of the visiting delegates.
Thanking you.
Yours Sincerely.

(V.Pirabakaran)
Leader
Liberation Tigers of Tamil Eelam

11th October 1994

Mr. V. Pirabakaran
Leader
Liberation Tigers of Tamil Eelam
LTTE Headquarters
Jaffna

Dear Mr. Pirabakaran,

I thank you for your letter dated 8th October 1994, addressed to my Hon. Prime Minister in reply to her letter dated 6th October, 1994. As suggested in your letter, our Delegation will arrive in Jaffna by helicopter in the morning of 13th October at 09.00a.m.

It is proposed that the heli-pad be marked by a large sized 'H' colored in white.

The proposed agenda for the discussion is as follows:

1. The transport of essential items and the distribution and supply of these items at the lowest possible prices.

2. Supply of electricity and the repair of roads, irrigation facilities, schools and hospital buildings.

3. Re-construction of the Jaffna library.

4. Exploration of the possibilities of the cessation of hostilities leading to a cease-fire.

5. Any other matters of importance.

We would welcome your agenda before our departure. Looking forward to meeting you in Jaffna.

Thanking you.
With kind regards.
Yours Sincerely

K. Balapatabendi
Secretary to the Prime Minister

Economic Blockade as Central Issue

The government agenda dealt with the transport and distribution of essential items. But the crucial issue of lifting the economic embargo was conveniently ignored. Although the new government partially lifted the sanctions on a few items, they did not reach the Tamil population in the North. The Sri Lankan military personnel guarding the border posts at Thandikulam imposed their own blockade on the lifted items. The economic blockade, similar to that which was imposed on Biafra by the Nigerian authorities in the sixties, had worsened the economic plight and made the conditions of existence of our people miserable and primitive. Several essential items, indispensable for daily existence, i.e. soap, cooking oil, boxes of matches etc. were banned. To our people, who were forced to live in darkness without electricity, items such as candles and torch batteries were prohibited. Such was the absurdity of the blockade.

Though 'security concerns' of the military were the underlying rationale behind the economic embargo and other bans, the whole enterprise became irrational and inhuman when more than 100 items without any relevance to military interests were included in the list of tabooed goods. For example, umbrellas, shoe polish, towels, shirts, trousers, printing paper, typing paper, wooden planks, printing machines, cycles, school bags, gold, tyres, spare parts of motor vehicles, electric cookers and several other items of no military significance were banned in Tamil areas. Though petrol, diesel, kerosene, engine oil, were banned so as to paralyse the mobility of the LTTE forces, it had no effect on the Tiger's war effort. But the civilian population suffered. Without energy, the economic life of the Tamil nation was in chaos. All fertilizers containing nitrogen and urea were banned simply because the military feared that explosives could be produced from them. This was a ludicrous measure, since the LTTE always had a plentiful supply of high powered explosives. But the ban had a devastating impact on agriculture and Tamil farmers suffered enormously. Fishing was banned in the northeastern waters ostensibly because the Sri Lankan navy feared that the Sea Tigers were active on the seas. The ban did not impede the maritime power of the Sea Tigers but it resulted in the slaughter of hundreds of innocent Tamil fishermen and the collapse of the Tamil fishing industry. The ban was imposed on cement and iron since the military did not want the Tigers to build bunkers to protect themselves from aerial and artillery bombardments. But the LTTE did build their bunkers. But the civilian properties that faced monumental destruction in the Tamil homeland could not be restored without cement and iron.

The economic blockade and other bans and restrictions imposed under the cover of 'security measures' did not affect or undermine the armed resistance of the LTTE. These measures denied the Tamil civilian population essential needs and caused them untold suffering. The economic repression was an essential part of the military strategy of the previous government to dominate and subjugate the Tamil people. Though starvation as a method of combat to subjugate a people blatantly violated international humanitarian law, the government kept the world in darkness by rigorous censorship that drew an iron curtain over the tragedy faced by the Tamil nation. We hoped that we could seek redress from the new government.

Because of the intensity of the suffering of our people as a consequence of these prolonging bans and embargoes, we decided to place the problem as the central issue on our agenda for talks. Mr. Pirabakaran insisted that we should pressurize the new government to remove the economic sanctions totally ahead of political negotiations. If Chandrika was genuine and sincerely concerned about the suffering of our people, she should undo the crimes committed by the UNP rulers, Mr.Pirabakaran argued.

We knew that Chandrika might encounter opposition from the military establishment if she dared to lift the ban on fuel and fertilizers. For the military hierarchy, the war was paramount and the bans served the interests of the military to prosecute the war. The sensible way to secure the removal of the sanctions without controversy was to effect a permanent cease-fire and bring an end to the war. Based on this premise, we decided to include the issue of cease-fire in the agenda for the preliminary discussions.

We deduced the complexity of the problems faced by our people into two levels: the existential and the political. The existential issues were the urgent, immediate, day to day problems caused by a set of bans and restrictions, which required utmost attention. The political problem was fundamental, relating to the rights and aspirations of our people, which required a thorough examination of causes to work out an acceptable solution. This would entail time.

Our strategy was to advance the peace process in progressive stages. We planned to discuss and resolve the urgent existential problems at the very early stages of the dialogue. We also wanted to press for a stable and permanent cease-fire in the preliminary discussions to end the war. A congenial environment of peace and normalcy was essential, we felt, before we entered into serious political negotiations. Our representatives were thoroughly briefed on our approach and strategy.

On the morning of the 13th of October 1994, Tamilselvan and myself were waiting at the open grounds of the Jaffna University to officially receive the government delegates. Massive crowds of jubilant people swarmed the venue. At 9 o'clock exactly, the helicopter carrying the government team landed on the marked spot. The delegates received a warm welcome from the Tigers as well as from the people of Jaffna. They were taken immediately to our political headquarters at Chundukuli, the venue of the meeting, escorted by armed LTTE cadres. At the political office we introduced them to our accredited representatives and the meeting commenced. I was made available for our representatives in the political office for consultation and guidance.

The first round of talks between the government delegation and the Liberation Tigers lasted for two days on the 13th and 14th of October 1994. It was a cordial meeting in which both the parties frankly articulated their respective positions. The LTTE delegates explained in depth and detail the immense suffering experienced by the Tamil civilian population as a consequence of the bans and restrictions and urged the government to lift the economic embargo totally. Our delegates insisted on the necessity of effecting a cease-fire to bring an end to the armed conflict. The removal of the economic sanctions and ending the war, our representatives emphasized, would pave the way for peace and normalization of civilian life. This was an essential condition for the negotiating process to succeed. Explaining the extreme hardships endured by our people to travel from the peninsula to the mainland, our delegates suggested the opening of the Sangupitty - Keerativu causeway for which the army camp at

Pooneryn had to be withdrawn. The government delegates gave a patient and sympathetic hearing and promised that authorities in Colombo would consider the issues discussed. No decisions were made, but an agreement was reached to resume the second round of talks within the next 10 days.

The Joint Statement

The following is the joint statement issued by the government delegation and the representatives of the Liberation Tigers of Tamil Eelam after the first round of talks held on 13th and 14th October 1994.

The first round of talks held between the Government of Sri Lankan and the Liberation Tigers of Tamil Eelam were conducted in an atmosphere of cordiality and good will. The talks were very constructive.

In his opening speech Mr. Karikalan, the leader of the LTTE's delegation said that the LTTE is committed to peace and peaceful settlement of the Tamil national question. 'Ever since the outbreak of hostilities in June 1990 the LTTE leadership has been calling for cessation of hostilities and peace talks. But the previous government had failed to take any positive steps to bring an end to the war and to open up negotiations. But we are glad to note that the new government of Chandrika Kumaratunga has taken constructive measures to create congenial conditions for peace. We are also pleased to note that she is genuinely committed to a political settlement through peaceful negotiations', Mr. Karikalan said.

'The collective aspirations of the Tamil people is to see an end to this war and the long standing suffering that resulted from this conflict. This war that was imposed on our people has caused tremendous suffering. The people are facing innumerable problems that are immediate and urgent. I think that the initial talks should address these problems. The LTTE fervently hopes that the Government should take urgent measures to redress the grievances of our people', Mr. Karikalan declared.

Mr. Karikalan emphasized the importance of cease-fire as a necessary condition for the creation of peaceful environment and for the return of normalcy. He also said that the stoppage of armed conflict will help to promote peace talks.

Welcoming the Government delegation to the negotiating table, Mr. Karikalan said that the LTTE will participate in these talks with an open mind and make every effort to co-operate with the government to make the talks successful.

The leader of the Government team Mr.K.Balapatabendi in his opening speech said, 'My colleagues and I have come here at the personal behest of the Prime Minister. She has asked us, first, to convey her warm greetings to you and to all the people of the North. She has also mandated us to discuss with you how best the Government can alleviate the hardships of daily life presently experienced by the people, both in terms of the enhanced supply of essential goods, as well as the restoration of services and repair of damaged utilities. We are further empowered to discuss with you ways of reducing the incidence of armed hostilities, with a view of achieving conditions conducive to an eventual cease-fire'.

Mr. Balapatabendi said that the existing situation in the North has become a national problem, and it requires for its definitive resolution. The Prime Minister therefore considers it important that a negotiated process be quickly launched which could successfully lead to the speedy establishment of peace, he declared.

"On this occasion our purpose is two-fold. At one level, we seek to discuss with you how best the government can ensure the adequate supply and equitable distribution of the essentials of life to all the people of the North. As a corollary of that, we seek to discuss with you how we may best advance the fulfillment of the State's overriding responsibility to provide to all segments of its citizenry, the public utilities and services which are essential to the community's well being", Mr. Balapatabendi explained.

"Therefore, in terms of a negotiated political settlement, our mandate is very much one of ascertaining the views of the LTTE and the people of the North in regard to the shape of national polity which they would wish to see. To that extent, we are here to listen to you, obtain clarifications, etc.

The Prime Minister is most gratified that her commitment to the peaceful resolution of our national problem without pre-conditions has been reciprocated by the LTTE and the Tamil community. She hopes accordingly, that this 'spirit of peace' can be realised henceforth through a conscious and monitored process to eliminate armed hostilities.

High expectations attaches to our shared venture: it behoves us therefore to manifest patience, understanding and flexibility in our talks. We assure you of our best effort to that end, and we look to you for reciprocity. My team and I are now ready, my friends, to engage in as wide-ranging a discussion as may be felt necessary. We can only hope that such discussion will lead us to the positive outcome of agreed practical arrangements which will above all else, serve the wellbeing of all the Tamil people, and the whole country", Mr. Balapatabendi said.

The talks were based on the agenda prepared by the Government delegation which focused mainly on the issues and problems faced by the people of the North.

On the question of transporting essential items and distributing them at low prices to the people, the LTTE representatives explained in detail the delays and difficulties involved in the movement of traffic at Thandikulam. They also pointed out that shipping rates on goods transported by seas have increased the prices. The Government delegation assured that necessary steps would be taken to remove the impediments in the flow of traffic at Thandikulam and also would take action to reduce or remove shipping charges.

On the question of opening up a land route between the Peninsula and the mainland, the LTTE delegates insisted on opening up the Sangupitty causeway for which they argued that the troops stationed at Pooneryn have to be withdrawn. The LTTE team further explained that the opening of this land route will facilitate the traffic of people and goods and that it would be considered as an act of goodwill towards the people of Jaffna. The Government delegates gave a sympathetic hearing and said that the matter would be taken into consideration.

On the question of economic reconstruction of the North, the Government delegates stated that the new administration of the Prime Minister Chandrika Kumaratunga has decided to take immediate steps to restore electricity, renovate irrigation schemes, and repair roads, schools and hospitals. The LTTE delegates gave details of the targets which needed urgent reconstruction. The LTTE assured that it would fully co-operate with the Government in the deployment of administrative and technical staff involved in the task of economic reconstruction.

On the request of the LTTE's delegation the government's team agreed to set up a commission of inquiry to investigate and report on the destruction of the Jaffna library. The Government's delegation also agreed to reconstruct the library.

The LTTE delegates emphasised the importance of cease-fire to create a congenial condition of peace and goodwill. The Government delegates argued that the possibilities for the cessation of hostilities have to be explored before the declaration of ceasefire. The Government delegates finally agreed to discuss the matter with the Defence authorities.

In conclusion, both parties agreed to resume the second round of talks within the next ten days.

(S.KARIKALAN)	*(K.BALAPATABENDI)*
Leader,	*Leader,*
LTTE delegation	*Government delegation*

Chandrika seemed pleased with the warm and friendly welcome accorded to her representatives by the Tamil Tigers, as well as by the Tamil population in Jaffna. On the 21 October 1994 she wrote a letter thanking Mr. Pirabakaran for the reception and hospitality and fixed the date for the second round of talks on 24th October 1994. The following is the text of the letter.

21st October 1994

Mr. V. Pirabakaran
Leader
Liberation Tigers of Tamil Eelam
LTTE Headquarters
Jaffna

Dear Mr. Pirabakaran,

I write to thank you and say how much we appreciate the warm welcome and hospitality you and your party extended to our Government Delegation when they visited Jaffna on the 13th and 14th October 1994.

We were pleased to note that the discussions were very cordial and that we were able to reach some conclusions regarding the reconstruction of the Jaffna Peninsula. We agree that the next round of talks take place on 24th October 1994.

Our delegation led by my Secretary, Mr. K. Balapatabendi would visit Jaffna on that day. We could talk further about the important matters that were discussed on the last day, including matters pertaining to the opening of a convenient route to Jaffna for the transportation of essential commodities and for the use of the public.

I hope that we could together arrive at the necessary solutions in order to realise the dream of peace, prosperity and justice, so cherished by all of our people. You can count on our fullest cooperation in your endeavors for peace.

The helicopter carrying our Delegation together with two

photographers namely: Mr. Palitha Wijesinghe and Mr. Sarath Dharmasire will arrive at the Jaffna University grounds around 8.15 a.m., and the Delegation will leave Jaffna at 5.00 p.m. the same day, 24th October 1994.
With kind regards.
Yours sincerely.

Chandrika Bandaranaike Kumaratunga
Prime Minister

On the 23rd of October 1994, the day before the second round of talks, Mr. Gaminini Dissanayake, the Opposition leader and the UNP's presidential candidate, was killed by a suicide bomber at an election rally in Colombo. The UNP leaders accused the LTTE of the assassination. The Government did not rush to blame the Tigers, but ordered an investigation. The LTTE, on its part, neither claimed responsibility nor denied it. Posters appeared in Colombo suburbs accusing the government and LTTE of a conspiracy in the murder. It was widely speculated in the Tamil political circles that the assassination was carried out by the LTTE for the central role played by Gamini Dissanayake in burning down the Jaffna Public Library in 1981, reducing to ashes 90,000 volumes of invaluable and irreplaceable historical books and archives - a deed condemned as an act of cultural genocide against the Tamils.

When the UNP openly accused the LTTE of the assassination and floated a conspiracy theory involving the PA administration, the government was compelled to suspend the peace talks to pacify the critics. Nevertheless, Chandrika, with an eye on the forthcoming Presidential elections, did not wish to jeopardize her electoral prospects by jettisoning her peace initiative. Kumaratunga continued to campaign for peace and an end to war and sought a mandate from all sections of the population to continue the peace process. The widow of Gamini Dissanayake, Srima

Dissanayake, contested as the UNP Presidential candidate.

In the Presidential elections on the 9th of November 1994, Chandrika Kumaratunga secured an overwhelming victory, obtaining over 62 per cent of the votes. The majority of the people gave her a solid mandate for peace. Addressing the nation, Chandrika declared, "the verdict of our people in the recent elections leaves me in no doubt of the depth and intensity of their desire and commitment to peace. This must be, however, peace with honor for both parties to the conflict for it to be strong and durable".

Contradictions
In Perceptions

Chandrika took the oath as President on 12th November 1994. As a gesture of good-will to mark the assumption to power of Kumaratunga as the new President, the LTTE unilaterally declared a cessation of hostilities for a week from 12th November to 19th November 1994. We communicated our decision to the government through the ICRC. There was no immediate response from the government.

While the LTTE fighters observed peace for the week, ceasing all armed actions, the Sri Lankan armed forces engaged in a series of hostile military actions. Civilian targets were also shelled and bombed causing civilian casualties. In one incident at Nedunkerni in Vanni, LTTE fighters were ambushed by the Sri Lankan troops and one of our senior military commanders Lt. Col. Amudan was killed and decapitated. The LTTE made an appeal through the ICRC requesting the return of his severed head. But the troops turned down our request. The incident made Mr. Pirabakaran dismayed and resentful.

On the 19th November 1994, Col. Ratwatte sent a brief message to Mr. Pirabakaran informing him of the government's willingness to declare a cessation of hostilities for two weeks with immediate effect. We give below the texts of the letters exchanged between Col. Ratwatte and Mr. Pirabakaran.

19th November 1994

Dear Mr. Prabhakaran,

We understand that the LTTE had declared a cessation of hostilities for a period of 07 days from 12th – 19th November. We regret that the decision to declare cessation of hostilities was not conveyed to us by you. We were informed about it indirectly by the ICRC on the 16th November.

Our government is prepared to declare a cessation of hostilities for an initial period of two weeks, commencing with immediate effect, providing you are willing to reciprocate by observing a cessation of hostilities on your part.

We would be thankful for an immediate reply.

With kind regards.
Yours Sincerely.

Anuruddha Ratwatte
Deputy Minister of Defence
Minister for Irrigation & Power.

LTTE Headquarters
Jaffna
20.11.1994

Col. Anurudda Ratwatte
Deputy Minister for Defence
Minister for Irrigation and Power
Sri Lanka.
Dear Col. Ratwatte,

Thank you very much for your communication dated 19.11.1994. I wish to inform you that we are giving an earnest and careful consideration to your proposal for a cessation of hostilities for a period of two weeks.

As you are aware, the LTTE declared a cessation of hostilities for seven days (from 12th to 19th November) as a gesture of goodwill to mark the assumption of power of the P.A. government. I should point out that our unilateral declaration of peace was leaked to the local and international media by your government intelligence agency even before we made our decision public. Furthermore, we have also confirmed to you our peace initiative through the ICRC.

Unfortunately, during this week of peace when LTTE ceased all armed hostilities, the Government forces undertook a series of hostile actions against the LTTE as well as against Tamil civilians, which saddened and disappointed us. In one incident, which took place in Nedunkerni area, one of our senior commanders Lt. Col. Amudan (Malli) was killed in an army ambush and decapitated. Our request for the return of his head, made through the ICRC, was also turned down by your forces. We view this incident as an extremely provocative action aimed to undermine our gesture for peace. Therefore, we kindly request you to hold an immediate investigation into this incident and inform us about the details.

We will inform you about our decision on the proposed cessation of hostilities as soon as we hear from you about the Nedunkerni incident.

With kind regards.
Yours Sincerely

(V.Pirabakaran)
Leader,
Liberation Tigers of Tamil Eelam

22th November 1994

Mr. V. Pirabhakaran,
Leader,
LTTE
Jaffna.

Dear Mr. Pirabhakaran,

I write with reference to your letter dated 20th November 1994.

I was very much perturbed to learn of the incident of 17th November at Nedunkerni as described by you in your letter.

A message had been received from Mr. Tamil Selvan on 18th November through ICRC to Secretary/Defence, quote

"Thursday 17.11.94 in the morning, two members of the LTTE were ambushed by the Sri Lanka Army near Koddakernal, Mullaitivu District.

During the incident, a senior member of the LTTE, Lt. Col. Malli, was killed. His body was mutilated by the SLA patrol and his head cut off. The SLA patrol left the place and took the head with them.

The LTTE is quote furious and sad unquote about this incident and has two very urgent requests:

1. The head of Mr. Malli should be returned immediately for decent burial:

2. Some explanation should be given.

Mr. Tamil Selvan is expecting a reply through ICRC before the end of the afternoon, Friday 18.11.94 "unquote.

Secretary/ Defence has sent a reply through ICRC the same day, quote

"Reference you FAX dated 18.11.1994 transmitting the information received from Mr. Tamil Selvan, Head of the political wing of the LTTE.

Deeply concerned to learn of this barbaric act. Have instructed Brigade Commander to inquire and report on this incident.

The head, if located early, could be returned. Otherwise ashes would be returned unquote.

I am informed that the head referred to in your letter had been in an advanced state of decomposition and as such was duly cremated.

Discussions are now in progress to hand over the ashes to ICRC at Vavuniya.

On receipt of message referred to above, Secretary/Defence has taken immediate action to set up a military court of inquiry under the Army Act to inquire into this incident. The court is proceeding with the inquiry. On the findings of this court appropriate action would be taken.

I consider it judicious to keep this communication confidential for the time being.

Anuruddha Ratwatte
Minister of Irrigation
Power & Energy and
Deputy Minister of Defence

LTTE Headquarters
Jaffna
25.11.1994

Col. Anurudda Ratwatte
Deputy Minister of Defence,
Minister of Irrigation, Power and Energy
Sri Lanka

Dear Col. Ratwatte,

Thank you very much for your letter dated 22nd Nov. 1994.

We are pleased to note that having realized the serious nature of the incident at Nedunkerni you have taken immediate action to set up a military court of inquiry. We are confident that on the findings of the court appropriate disciplinary action will be taken against the perpetrator of this heinous act.

> *We have given serious thought to your proposal for a bilateral cessation of hostilities for two weeks. While appreciating your gesture, we are of the opinion that temporary declarations of cease-fires would serve little purpose to promote stable peace unless modalities are worked out to ensure strict observation of cessation of armed hostilities. We, therefore, suggest that the matter of cessation of armed hostilities and the modalities for which should be given detailed discussion at the negotiating table before making an official announcement. We hope that you will consider our suggestion favorably.*
>
> *Thanking you.*
> *With kind regards.*
> *Yours Sincerely.*
>
>
> *(V.Pirabakaran)*
> *Leader*
> *Liberation Tigers of Tamil Eelam*

Mr. Pirabakaran was not in favor of a short-lived temporary cessation of hostilities, but rather he wanted a stable, permanent cease-fire supervised by an international monitoring committee. It was precisely for that reason Mr. Pirabakaran called for detailed discussion on the procedures and modalities of the truce.

A Provocative Letter From Ratwatte

Col. Ratwatte, in his reply to the LTTE leader on 7th December 1994, distinguished between cessation of hostilities and cease-fire arguing that 'the former could be a prelude to the latter'. A cessation of hostilities, in his conception, was less formal and binding than a cease-fire. From his letter we could deduce that the government favored a temporary cessation of hostilities not a stable, permanent cease-fire. Col. Ratwatte also linked the cessation of hostilities to political negotiations and insisted that political negotiations should commence immediately, following the declaration of the truce. The concluding part of the letter was cleverly crafted propaganda material that attempted to boost the image of Chandrika as a courageous leader committed to peace while it blamed the LTTE for 'systematically massacring all the leaders of the Sinhala people in addition to all the Tamil leaders who opposed the LTTE'. Writing in a condescending and bitter tone, Ratwatte claimed that Chandrika was accused of being 'too lenient' with the organisation responsible for such crimes. Yet, Ratwatte boasted that the government took 'immense political risk' by resuming the dialogue with the LTTE. Ratwatte also praised the Sinhala people by heaping 'eternal credit' on them for not succumbing to racist pressures instigated by the Opposition. The concluding paragraphs denigrated both the LTTE and the UNP while commending the government for its 'unshaking vision of peace'. The letter contained all the ammunition to be used in a propaganda war in case the talks failed. The following is the full text of the letter:

7th December 1994

Mr. V. Pirabhakaran
Leader, LTTE
Jaffna.

Dear Mr. Prabhakaran,

I write with reference to your letter dated 25th December 1994.

First, I wish to recall the sequence of events, which have underlined the efforts of our Government to open up and carry forward the peace process.

Within two weeks of our Party taking over the reins of government, in August 1994, the Hon. Prime Minister, Mrs. Chandrika Bandaranaike Kumaratunga, decided to lift the embargo on 28 items. She addressed a letter to you immediately afterwards commencing a dialogue which continued through several letters written by her and replies sent you, eventually leading to the visit of our Government's Peace Delegation to Jaffna on the 13th and 14th of October. The warm and cordial reception of the delegation by the people and the LTTE was appreciated by us.

As you know, the first round of talks dealt only with the reconstruction and repair of the war torn areas in the North East, the opening up of a route to and from Jaffna, etc.

The LTTE gave us specific requests regarding priorities for reconstruction. At the second round of talks, our delegation was to present to the LTTE, details of projects the Government would undertake. This included most of your requests.

The assassination of the Leader of the Opposition and the Opposition's main candidate for the then ongoing Presidential campaign, just six hours before the departure of our delegation to Jaffna for the second round of talks, obliged us to postpone the event.

I suppose you are also aware that soon after this, we were fully involved in the presidential election and urgent attendant matters of State.

It is during this time we learnt that the LTTE had, on instructions, declared a cessation of hostilities for one week starting from the 12th of November; the day Mrs. Kumaratunga took oath as the President of Sri Lanka.

In the absence of any official intimation by the LTTE of a rumored cessation of hostilities, the government sought clarification through the ICRC, and was informed that there actually was a cessation of hostilities only on the evening of the 16th of October, just one day before you called it off. I wish to inform you once again that the Government cannot respond to hearsay of informal information – it can only respond to official knowledge.

In response to your declaration of the cessation of hostilities, we wrote to you on the 19th of November proposing a cessation of hostilities for an initial period of 2 weeks, provided the LTTE would agree to cease hostilities on their part.

You replied that you would inform us of your decision regarding our proposal for a cessation of hostilities after the Government *investigation into the unfortunate incident at Nedunkerni, where LTTE Commander Arundan was killed by the Amy.*

We received your letter dated November 20th on the 22nd of November and replied on the same day indicating that we had appointed a Military Court of Inquiry to investigate the incident at Nedunkerni.

You replied on the 25th of November, which we received on the 26th of November, expressing your pleasure at our decision. You also stated therein that 'the matter of cessation of armed hostilities and modalities for it should be given detailed discussion at the negotiating table, before making an official announcement'.

We are in agreement to discuss the modalities of a cessation of hostilities, but we would like to obtain your views about certain fundamental issues, without which, discussing details about a cessation of hostilities would be meaningless.

I set these out briefly -

(1) Whether the LTTE agrees in principle to a cessation of hostilities.

(2) We see a cessation of hostilities as a direct prelude to commencing negotiations between the Government and the LTTE in order to end conflict and to arrive at political solutions to the problems which caused the war.

(3) A cessation of hostilities should not be confused with a ceasefire.

The former could be a prelude to the latter.

A cessation of hostilities is less formal and binding than a ceasefire.

During a cessation of hostilities, both parties remain frozen in their positions as at present, while remaining fully armed and alert.

Neutral observers may be invited to monitor the process if both sides so desire.

Details regarding the effective implementation of a cessation could be agreed upon across a negotiating table, once agreement is reached re the above points.

(4) During the entire peace process, the LTTE must refrain from all political assassinations anywhere in the Island.

(5) We hope we will be able to arrive at an agreement about the cessation of hostilities within the next two weeks and then commence the actual peace negotiations soon after.

(6) We are ready to commence some of the reconstruction work and the opening of a roadway to Jaffna as discussed with you. We shall send a detailed report of it to you by the end of this week and shall be glad to receive your response soon.

In concluding my letter, it is opportune to mention that a massive effort to stir up racial hatred was set in motion by some elements within the UNP and other opponents, stating the fact that it was our Government's commencement of the peace process which gave the LTTE the possibility of assassinating Sinhala leaders, etc., etc.

The personal credibility of our leader, Mrs. Kumaratunga, was put directly into question before the entire nation. The major and almost exclusive election platform of the UNP and several other candidates was the issue of Mrs. Chandrika Bandaranaike Kumaratunga being too lenient with the LTTE which was shown up as the organisation responsible for systematically massacring all the leaders of the Sinhala people, in addition to all the Tamil leaders who opposed the LTTE. The PA Government was said to betray the Sinhala people by talking to the LTTE. It is to the credit of our government that we withstood all pressures to halt the peace process. We possess a clear and unshaking vision of peace for our country - yours and mine, and a lasting desire to build a nation where all our peoples could live in freedom, dignity, equality, coupled with the sincerity and courage to implement it, in the face of all obstacles.

We took the grave risk, politically and personally, of continuously stating that we had only temporarily suspended the talks, but that the peace process would continue. It is to the eternal credit of the Sinhala people that they did not succumb to the many racist pressures.

They have given our government and our President a massive mandate against racial hatred and discrimination and for peace.

The Sinhala people, together with the Tamils and Muslims of Sri Lanka, have in one voice called upon our government and have placed their faith in us to solve the problems of the North and East.

Within three weeks after the suspension of the talks, due to the tensions that ensued after the assassination of 53 persons on the night of 23rd October, our government had the courage to re-open a dialogue with yourself and the LTTE, fully aware of the immense political risk that may await us. This is because we are committed to the cause of peace. We sincerely hope that your commitment is of the same order and that together we could end this tragic war and establish Peace and Prosperity for our peoples.

Thanking you,
With kind regards,
Yours sincerely,

Col. Anuraddha Ratwatte
Deputy Minister of Defence

Ratwatte's letter was sarcastic and provocative. Mr. Pirabakaran was annoyed. He wanted to send a strongly worded letter to Ratwatte accusing Sinhala political leaders, both dead and alive, of genocide, of slaughtering sixty thousand innocent Tamils, a phenomenon still continuing under the cover of war and economic strangulation. I advised Mr. Pirabakaran not to respond emotionally but to deal with these issues with political sagacity. He concurred.

From the content of Ratwatte's letter, the LTTE leadership realised that the Kumaratunga government had taken a firm and entrenched position on specific issues. It was evident that the government was not in favor of a stable, permanent cease-fire but rather favored a temporary cessation of hostilities. The government was also opposed to the movement of the negotiating process in progressive stages as proposed by the LTTE. In other words, the government was not in favor of addressing and resolving what the LTTE characterized as urgent existential problems. Rather, the government wanted to open up political negotiations immediately with the declaration of a cessation of hostilities. The reluctance shown by the government to lift the economic sanctions, to open a land route to the mainland and to remove the ban on fishing could only be attributed to the ascendancy of militarism in the new government. Kumaratunga's regime accorded primacy to the strategic interests of the military, ignoring the existential plight of the Tamil civilian masses. Disillusioned with the government's attitude and approach, the Tamil Tigers had also firmly resolved to assert their own position. In essence, Ratwatte's letter effectively contributed to the widening of the gap between the negotiating parties.

On the 8th of December 1994, the LTTE's leader dispatched the following letter to Col. Ratwatte.

LTTE Headquarters
Jaffna
8.12.1994

Col. Anuruddha Ratwatte,
Minister for Irrigation and Power,
Deputy Minister for Defence,
Sri Lanka
Dear Col. Ratwatte,

I am pleased to receive your letter dated 7th December 1994.

Your letter explains in some detail the position of your government with regard to the peace process and sets out certain specifications on the question of cessation of hostilities and negotiations.

We do appreciate the manner in which your government faced and withstood the challenges posed by racist elements to undermine the process of peace negotiations. In spite of the malicious disinformation campaign launched against the LTTE, we are pleased to note that the wider sections of the Sinhala people opted for peace and have given your Government an overwhelming mandate to carry forward the process of negotiations and to seek a solution to the ethnic conflict by peaceful means.

You will appreciate that from the outset the LTTE has been insisting that the initial stages of the negotiations should be given primacy to the immediate and urgent problems faced by our people. In the first round of talks, our delegation has specified these issues, which are mostly creations resulting from the military approach advanced by the previous regime. Though the government delegation pledged 'to alleviate the hardships of daily life presently experienced by the people', no action has been taken so far to redress the grievances of our people.

The urgent problems of our people cannot be reduced to 'some reconstruction and repair works'. There are far more pressing problems which have to be resolved to create genuine conditions of peace and normalization of civilian life in the war torn areas.

Even though your government is fully aware of these urgent issues, and has absolute authority to resolve these problems, there seems to be a reluctance to make any positive moves in this direction. We can attribute this to the Government's unwillingness to act contrary in anyway to the overall strategic interests and designs of the military. This approach of giving primacy to military interests over and above the existential concerns of a civilian population, I wish to point out, will pose serious obstacles when tackling the immediate and urgent issues faced by the Tamil people. This is already evidenced by the reluctance shown in lifting the economic embargo fully, in opening the Sangupitty causeway, in lifting the ban on the fishing zone etc.

I do not wish to elaborate these issues, since these matters will be brought to the negotiating table by our delegation when the second round of talks resumes in the near future. I should emphasize that the day to day problems of our people are of paramount importance and need urgent solutions and should be a prelude to discussions on basic issues underlying the Tamil national conflict.

In your letter, you have called for clarifications on certain issues, some of which, you will appreciate, have to be dealt with through direct dialogue. In our earlier communications, we referred to cease-fire to mean total cessation of armed hostilities. Yet, you have explained cessation of hostilities as a process leading to cease-fire or rather, the former should be a prelude to the latter. Without entering into a conceptual debate, we have decided to proceed on the basis of your distinction.

The LTTE agrees in principle to a cessation of hostilities. If the Government makes an official declaration of a cessation of hostilities for an initial period of two weeks, as you have proposed, the LTTE will reciprocate by observing the same. The modalities and effective implementation of the cessation of hostilities should be discussed and agreed upon at the negotiating table. We have always insisted that a condition of peace should be a prelude to peace negotiations.

We are committed to peace and we fervently hope that the process of negotiations will lead to a permanent peace and to the resolution of the ethnic conflict.

Thanking you.
With kind Regards.
Yours Sincerely.

(V.Pirabakaran)
Leader
Liberation Tigers of Tamil Eelam

In a brief but conciliatory letter sent to Pirabakaran on 13th December 1994 Col. Ratwatte assured him that the existential day to day problems of the Tamil people would be resolved 'to the best of our ability'. While indicating the government's willingness to declare a cessation of hostilities on the 1st January 1995 for an initial period of 2 weeks, he proposed that the government delegation would visit Jaffna on the 21st or 22nd of December. Following are texts of Col. Ratwatte's letters and Mr. Pirabakaran's response:

December 13,1994

Mr. V. Pirabhakaran
Leader
LTTE
Jaffna.
Dear Mr. Pirabhakaran,

Thank you for you letter dated December 8, 1994.

We have noted your views regarding Peace, the militarisation of the ethnic problem and the well being of the Tamil people, with great interest. We wish to assure you that our lasting concern for the 'day-to-day problems of the Tamil people and of our commitment to solve them to the best of our ability, with your fullest co-operation. The details concerning all these matters could be discussed at negotiations.

We are glad that you have agreed to reciprocate by observing a cessation of hostilities if the Government makes an official declaration of same.

We are willing to declare a cessation of hostilities on the 1st January 1995, for an initial period of 2 weeks. We will intimate same to you by letter while announcing it to the media.

We request the LTTE to reciprocate by declaring a cessation of hostilities on your part and intimating same to the Government by letter and if you desire, announcing it publicly.

If you agree to the above proposal, the Government is prepared to send a delegation to Jaffna to discuss the modalities of implementation of the cease-fire, before declaring the cessation of hostilities.

We suggest that the delegation could go to Jaffna on Wednesday the 21st or Thursday the 22nd of December. You have stated that 'a condition of Peace should be a prelude to Peace negotiations'. We take it that what you mean by a 'condition of Peace' is a cessation of hostilities between the two parties. As stated in my last letter, I cannot agree more with you that the Government cannot enter into Peace talks with the LTTE while hostilities continue.

We appreciate your commitment to Peace. I am sure you are aware that we have consistently stated our firm commitment to Peace.

We believe that it is now time to keep the country informed of the recent developments in our dialogue. We, therefore, propose to release the relevant information to the Press after you receive this letter.

Thanking you,
With kind regards,
Yours Sincerely,

Col. Anuruddha Ratwatte
Deputy Minister of Defence
Minister for Irrigation, Power & Energy

LTTE Headquarters
Jaffna
15th December 1994

Col. Anuruddha Ratwatte,
Deputy Minister of Defence
Minister of Irrigation, Power and Energy
Sri Lanka.

Dear Col. Ratwatte,

Thank you for your letter dated 13th December 1994.

We are impressed and encouraged by your assurance that the immediate and urgent issues facing the Tamil people will be given primacy and resolved. This is crucial for the restoration of a peaceful environment and for the normalization of civilian life.

We are pleased to note that you are willing to declare a cessation of hostilities on the 1st of January 1995, for an initial period of two weeks. We wish to assure you that we will reciprocate by observing a cessation of hostilities during that period once you make an official declaration and intimate the same to us by letter. The LTTE will also make a similar declaration and inform you.

You will appreciate that a detailed discussion clarifying the procedures and modalities of the implementation of the cease-fire is vial before the declaration of cessation of hostilities. We are glad to note that you are prepared to send a delegation to Jaffna to discuss this issue. The Government delegation is welcome to Jaffna either on the 21st or 22nd of December as is convenient to them. Please confirm the date of arrival and the names and details of the Government delegates.

Thanking you.
Yours Sincerely.

(V.Pirabakaran)
Leader,
Liberation Tigers of Tamil Eelam

In his communication dated 19th December 1994, Ratwatte reasserted the government's position that peace negotiations should commence soon after the cessation of hostilities.

Ratwatte's communications to the LTTE leader clearly indicated that the government considered cessation of hostilities as a conciliatory gesture or rather a concession granted in exchange for the participation of the LTTE in the political dialogue. Therefore, cessation of war was inextricably linked to the commencement of talks. Both are fundamental matters, Ratwatte pointed out from his earlier communication without which discussing details about a cessation of hostilities would be meaningless. Ratwatte demanded an assurance from Mr. Pirabakaran whether he would be ready for talks once a cessation of hostilities was declared. Following was the text of the letter.

December 19,1994

Mr. V. Pirabhakaran,
Leader
LTTE
Jaffna.

Dear Mr. Pirabhakaran,

I thank you for your letter dated December 16, 1994 and for agreeing to welcome the Government delegation to Jaffna.

As stated by me in my letter of December 13,1994, we are ready to send a delegation to Jaffna to discuss the modalities of the cessation of hostilities, as agreed upon by us.

I had invited your attention to several crucial points in my letter of December 7, 1994. You have responded to some of these in your reply dated December 9, 1994. But I note that you have not expressed your views with regard to Points (2) and (5), where I clearly stated that we see a cessation of hostilities 'as a direct prelude to commencing negotiations' for peace. I also stated therein that we hoped peace negotiations could commence soon after the cessation of hostilities. In page 2 of the same letter, I mentioned that we wished to obtain your views about these points, which were 'fundamental matters without which discussing details about cessation of hostilities would be meaningless'.

I would be grateful to have your assurance that immediately after a cessation of hostilities is declared, you would be ready to enter into peace negotiations aimed at 'ending the armed conflict and to arrive at a political solution for the problems which caused the war'.

On hearing from you regarding these matters, the Government delegation would be ready to leave immediately to Jaffna for discussions, even on the 22nd December as suggested by us, or on later date between the 27th and 30th December, if you find this convenient.

*Thanking you,
With our best wishes,
Yours sincerely,*

*Anuruddha Ratwatte
Minister of Irrigation, Power & Energy and
Deputy Minister of Defence*

The LTTE leader was displeased and dismayed over the government's strategy of linking the proposed temporary cessation of hostilities with political negotiations. In a strongly worded letter to Col. Ratwatte, Mr. Pirabakaran reiterated the LTTE's position. The urgent existential issues that arose 'as consequential effects of the military offensive operations of the state against our people' should be addressed and resolved in the early stages of the peace talks, he re-asserted. Quoting the assurances given by Mr. Balapatabendi, the leader of the government's peace delegation and

Col. Ratwatte, LTTE's leader charged the government of a deliberate shift in position aimed at 'circumventing the most crucial and immediate issues that beset our people today'. Concluding the letter, Mr. Pirabakaran pointed out there was widespread anticipation among the Tamil people that the new government would fulfil its commitment and any attempt to side track these issues would be considered by the LTTE and Tamils 'as an act of political bad faith'. Here below we publish the full text of Mr. Pirabakaran's letter.

LTTE Headquarters
Jaffna
21ˢᵗ December 1994

Col. Anuraddha Ratwatte
Deputy Minister of Defence
Minister of Irrigation, Power and Energy
Sri Lanka.

Dear Col. Ratwatte,

Thank you for your letter dated 19ᵗʰ December 1994, which reached us on the following day through the good offices of the ICRC.

In our letters dated 8.12.1994 and 15.12.1994 we have responded to your queries and clarified several issues. We have responded positively to your proposals for a cessation of hostilities and agreed to discuss the modalities of implementation before the declaration of ceasefire. You have agreed to our contention that the creation of a peaceful environment is conducive to peace negotiations. Complying to our view, you have stated in your letter dated 13.12.1994 that, "I cannot agree more with you that the Government cannot enter into peace talks with the LTTE while hostilities continue".

We have stated emphatically that we are committed to peace and "we fervently hope that the process of negotiations will lead to a permanent peace and to the resolution of the ethnic conflict". (see our letter dated 8.12.1994)

We expected that peace negotiations should commence soon after the declaration of cessation of hostilities. We have insisted from the very beginning and re-iterated over and over again that the initial stages of the peace negotiations should address the immediate and urgent issues faced by the Tamil people.

To clarify this point and to refresh your memory, may I quote a few paragraphs from our letter dated 8.12.1994. "You will appreciate that from the outset the LTTE has been insisting that the initial stages of the negotiations should give primacy to the immediate and urgent problems faced by our people. In the first round of talks, our delegation has specified these issues, which are mostly creations resulting from the military approach advanced by the previous regime. Though the government delegation pledged to 'alleviate the hardships of daily life presently experienced by the people' no action has been taken so far to redress the grievances of our people".

"....There are far more pressing problems, which have to be resolved to create genuine conditions of peace and normalisation of civilian life in the war torn areas".

".... I should emphasize that the day to day problems of our people are of paramount importance and need urgent solutions and should be a prelude to discussions on basic issues underlying the Tamil national conflict".

You will appreciate that what we have been insisting is that the most urgent issues that arose as a consequential effect of the military offensive operations of the State against our people should be addressed before we engage ourselves in analysing the root causes of the armed conflict.

The first round of talks, I wish to point out, was primarily concerned with those issues. The leader of the government team, Mr. K. Balapatabendi has said that they were mandated by the Prime Minister to discuss "how best the Government can alleviate the hardships of daily life presently experienced by the people". Though the Government delegation pledged to take immediate measures to provide "all utilities and services essential to the community's well being", no action has been taken to redress these grievances. We hoped that these matters would be taken up for discussion at the second round of talks.

You have also agreed to our view and appreciated our concerns when you stated in your letters dated 13th December 1994, that, "we wish to assure you of our lasting concern for the day today problems of the Tamil people and our commitment to solve them to the best of our ability, with your fullest co-operation".

Having obtained detailed clarifications of our views, and having given assurances that the immediate and urgent issues of our people will be given primacy in the peace negotiations, you have written to us again on the 19th December, commenting, to our dismay, that peace negotiations should be confined to the 'causes of war' aimed at 'ending the armed conflict'. From what you are insisting on now, we can deduce a deliberate shift in your position aimed at circumventing the most crucial and immediate issues that beset our people today which require immediate attention and resolution.

We are very clear in our view that the overall objective of the peace process should be aimed at resolving the national problem by exploring the causes of the armed conflict. We assure you that there is no differing perception on this fundamental issue. What we wish to emphasize is that the peace process should be advanced in stages. The early stages of the peace negotiations, we wish to reiterate, should address the pressing problems and hardships encountered by our people which are crucial for the restoration of normalcy and for the creation of a peaceful environment. This is the consensus view of the Tamil people, who have been entertaining the hope that the new government would bring them relief by alleviating their day to day issues. Since the first round of talks was predicated on this premise, and since your government pledged to give primacy to the urgent issues, there is a widespread expectation among our people that your Government will fulfil its commitments. Therefore, any attempts on the part of the Government to sidetrack or circumvent these issues would be considered by us and by our people as an act of political bad faith.

I think we have clarified our stand adequately. We hope that you will find our position fair, reasonable and pragmatic.

I wish to reiterate that we are committed to peace and that our doors for peace are open.

We are ready to receive the Government delegation in Jaffna at any date convenient to you.

Thanking you.
Yours sincerely.

(V. Pirabakaran)
Leader
Liberation Tigers of Tamil Eelam

In responding to Mr. Pirabakaran's strident letter, Col. Ratwatte denied the accusation that the government had shifted its position and was attempting to circumvent the most crucial and immediate issues. It was a deliberate misrepresentation of the situation, he argued. The Government was sincerely committed 'to provide the basic utilities for civil life, to restore normalcy in the northeast...' he said. Ratwatte also consented to the LTTE's approach that peace process should be advanced in stages and the early stages should be devoted to the resolution of the pressing problems and hardships of the Tamil people. The letter was written in a conciliatory tone. A date for the second round of direct talks was fixed to discuss the modalities of the cessation of hostilities. The following is the text of that correspondence.

December 29,1994

Mr. V. Pirabhakaran
Leader
LTTE
Jaffna

Dear Mr. Pirabhakaran,

I acknowledge with thanks your letter of 21st December 1994, transmitted to us through the good offices of the ICRC.

I wish to emphatically state that in my letter of 19th December, we requested a clarification of some specific points re the commencement of Peace talks, for the following reasons.

(a) In my letter sent to you in the first week of December, I set out several points, requesting your views. You had responded to several of these, but remained silent re points (2) and (5) which specified our government's views on the Peace negotiations. We stated therein that we clearly saw a cessation of hostilities as a prelude to Peace talks, which should commence immediately after a declaration of a cessation.

Your non-response re this crucial matter caused concern to our government. As you are aware, our government always believed that <u>the Peace Process should lead on to political negotiations, the final objective of which should be the meaningful political solution of the ethnic conflict</u>. This would obviously have to identify and alleviate 'the causes of the prevailing war', in order to 'end the armed conflict or the civil war'.

(b) This does not in any way change our Government's commitment to alleviate the hardships of daily life presently experienced by the people of the North-East as was stated by Mr. Bala patabendi, the leader of the Government delegation to Jaffna last October.

It is to this end that our Government lifted the embargo on 28 items considered essential for the daily life of the inhabitants of the North, within two weeks of assuming power.

It is also because of this policy that our delegation on their first visit to Jaffna, discussed matters re the amelioration of the civil life of the people. Matters such as the reconstruction of the North, the repair of roads, irrigation works, schools, hospitals, the supply of electricity, the opening of a roadway to and from Jaffna, etc. were discussed.

Your delegation specified certain priorities. At the second round of talks, our delegation was prepared to present the items which the Government could immediately undertake to implement. The delay in doing this was due to reasons beyond our control, as we stated in a previous letter to you. The mass assassinations of the Leader of the Opposition and over 50 others in Colombo, compelled us to suspend discussions with the LTTE.

We are surprised and disappointed that while being fully aware of these facts, you attempt to misrepresent the situation when you state in your letter that we are deliberately shifting our position with the intention of 'circumventing the most crucial and immediate issues that beset our people today.....' You also say that our Government took no action to redress the grievances of the people of the North.

I reiterate once more that our Government's commitment to provide the basic utilities for civil life, to restore normalcy to the North-East and to develop in the same manner as the rest of Sri Lanka, has not changed or lessened in any way.

To try to imply this is unjustified and could prove harmful to the mutual understanding that we are attempting to build up at such a cost and with so much difficulty.

(c) *The primary objective of our Government is to find a political solution to the ethnic problem, to end the armed conflict/ the war, and to establish lasting peace in our country, and build a new Sri Lanka where all its peoples - Sinhala Tamil, Muslim, burgher - could live as equal citizens with dignity and in peace and harmony.*

To find political solutions, we have to talk, to dialogue, to commence talks or negotiations.

(d) *The alleviation of the hardships faced by the people of the North-East, the cessation of armed hostilities between the Government and the LTTE, are all preliminaries - essential no doubt, which should simultaneously lead on to <u>the primary objective - which is the formulation of a political</u>*

package of solutions to end the war and to resolve the problem of the Tamil people of the North-East of Sri Lanka.

We insisted on receiving your response to this view of our Government as your views on this particular and crucial issue were not clearly stated in your correspondence with us.

In your reply to these issues, in your letter dated 22nd December, you express your views more specifically when you state that 'the peace process should be advanced in stages... the early stages.... should address the pressing problems and hardships encountered by our people....'etc.

As there seems to be agreement by us both on this issue, I propose the following for our future negotiations: -

(1) Our delegation could visit Jaffna on 2nd January 1995, for a one-day discussion.

(2) The discussion would take up the following major issues:-

    (i) a cessation of hostilities to be declared from the 7th or 8th January, 1995, for an initial period of two weeks. The modalities of the cessation of hostilities to be agreed upon.

    (ii) The work of reconstruction, opening up of a roadway, etc., aimed at ameliorating the conditions of daily life of the people of the North-East.

    (iii) Decide upon dates for the commencement of the 2nd part of the peace negotiations - i.e the discussion of the possible political solutions to the problems of the people of the North-East – i.e. issues re political power, the unit/s of administration and related matters.

I take this opportunity to wish you a happy 1995 that would usher in Peace and Prosperity to our country.

*Thanking you,
Yours sincerely.*

*Anuruddha Ratwatte
Minister of Irrigation, Power & Energy
Deputy Minister of Defence*

We were well aware that the ultimate objective of the peace process was to find a meaningful political settlement to the ethnic conflict. There was no doubt in our minds that we had to discuss and resolve the political issues underlying the armed conflict. However there was a total misreading in the government circles that the LTTE was avoiding political negotiations. That was a mistaken perception. What the LTTE wanted was a stable foundation to begin the process of political negotiations. The LTTE felt that it was crucial to create a congenial environment of peace and normalcy in Tamil areas as a necessary foundation to engage in a political dialogue. A peaceful environment could be established by a stable cease fire with international supervision and normalisation of civilian life could be achieved by the removal of all the bans and restrictions imposed on the Tamils. Ending the war and removing the oppressive constraints, we felt, would not only bring relief to the suffering masses but also would create a congenial atmosphere for political discussions. It was our concern that a permanent political settlement should satisfy the political aspirations of the Tamil people and also alleviate the apprehensions of the Sinhala masses. We knew this to be a difficult task. It would require a great deal of mutual dialogue; possibly over a long period of time. It was precisely for this reason we wanted the urgent day to day problems of the people to be addressed and resolved in the initial stages of the dialogue. The Tigers wanted to conduct the political negotiations 'in a free and unrestrained atmosphere' the LTTE leader pointed out in his reply to Ratwatte.

The following is the text of of Mr. Pirabakaran's reply:

LTTE Headquarters
Jaffna
1ˢᵗ January 1995

Col. Anuraddha Ratwatte
Minister of Irrigation, Power and
Energy
Deputy Minister of Defence
Sri Lanka

Dear Col. Ratwatte,

Thank you very much for your letter dated 29ᵗʰ December 1994.

I am pleased to note that you are in agreement with our view concerning the procedure of the peace process, i.e. that the negotiating process should be advanced in stages and that the early stages of the peace negotiations should address the immediate problems and hardships experienced by our people.

We appreciate your Government's commitment to ameliorate the conditions of existence of our people and to resolve the Tamil national conflict through peace negotiations. There has never been any misconception on our part that the fundamental objective of the peace process is to find a meaningful political solution that would satisfy the aspirations of the Tamil people.

You are fully aware that the Tamil people in the Northeast are undergoing extreme hardships as the direct consequence of the war and the hard-line militaristic approach advanced by the previous regime, the constraints and pressures of which have not yet been relaxed to create the conditions of normalcy in the war affected areas. The elimination of these constraints, we believe, will not only alleviate the hardships experienced by our people but also will create a congenial environment to conduct peace negotiations in a free and unrestrained atmosphere which is crucial for the success of the peace talks. Such a process of reconciliation is also necessary to build trust and confidence among the Tamil community which has been embittered by non-fulfillment of pledges and promises for decades. It is for these reasons, we placed emphasis on the resolution of the immediate, day to day issues, which are of paramount importance in relation to the existential conditions experienced by our people.

Our delegation will spell out in more detail and in depth such issues in the second round of talks and we hope that the Government will take concrete action to redress these grievances.

The Government delegation is welcome to Jaffna on the 2nd January 1995, as you have suggested, to conduct the second round of talks.

May I wish you a happy, peaceful and prosperous New Year.

Thanking you.
Yours Sincerely.

(V.Pirabakaran)
Leader
Liberation Tigers of Tamil Eelam

The second round of talks took place at the political headquarters of the LTTE in Jaffna on the 2nd of January 1995. This time the government team included a senior army officer Brigadier A.S Peris and a naval officer, Captain Prasanna Rajaratne. Mr. Tamilselvan, head of the political wing, led the LTTE delegation.

The discussions were primarily centred on the procedures, modalities, supervision and implementation of a cessation of hostilities. It was decided that armed combat formations of both parties should maintain present positions keeping a distance of 600 metres between them and freeze all hostile armed activities or offensive operations during cessation of hostilities.

The government delegation agreed to allow normal fishing except in specified areas i.e. the vicinity of naval bases and coastal military camps. Both the parties agreed to form monitoring committees to supervise and inquire into the violations of the terms of agreement. The committees would be appointed in all the Tamil districts in the Northeast and be chaired by foreign representatives. It was also decided that notice of termination of cessation of hostilities should be given at least 72 hours before termination. A brief seven point document was formulated during the talks specifying the terms and conditions of the truce agreement.

The formal declaration of the cessation of hostilities was signed simultaneously by both President Kumaratunga in Colombo and Mr. V.Pirabakaran in Jaffna and the document was exchanged between them by the good offices of the ICRC. The cessation of hostilities came into effect from 8th January 1995. The following was the declaration:

Declaration of Cessation of Hostilities

The modalities for the implementation of the agreed Cessation of Hostilities by the Government and the LTTE for a specified period will be as follows: -

1. **There will be no offensive operations by either party during this period. An offensive operation will be considered a violation of the agreement.**

2. **The Security Forces and the LTTE will maintain their present**

positions on the ground, keeping a minimum of 600 meters between each other. However, each party would reserve the right of movement within 100 meters from their own bunker lines, keeping a minimum of 400 meters in between. Any party moving in the restricted areas would be considered an offensive operation.

3. The Navy and the Air Force will continue to perform their legitimate tasks for safeguarding the sovereignty and territorial integrity of the country, from external aggression, without in anyway engaging in offensive operations against the LTTE, or causing any obstructions to legitimate and bonafide fishing in specified areas.

4. Acts such as sabotage, bomb explosions, abductions, assassinations and intimidations directed at any political group, party or individual will amount to an offensive operation.

5. a. It is suggested that Committees to deal with violations of this agreement be set up to inquire into any instances of violation of the above terms of agreement. These Committees could be set up in the areas of Jaffna, Mannar, Vavuniya, Mulaitivu, Trincomalee and Batticaloa-Amparai and any other areas as deemed necessary.

   b. It will be the responsibility of these Committees to take immediate action on complaints made by either party to this agreement to inquire into and resolve such disputes.

   c. These Committees could comprise representatives drawn from Canada, Netherlands, Norway, ICRC, and from among retired Judges or Public Officers, Religious Heads and other leading citizens; all appointed by mutual agreement.

d. Each Committee could consist of five members, viz:
   02 from Government;
   02 from L.T.T.E.;
   01 from a Foreign Country who will be Chairman.

e. Freedom of movement for the Committees to perform their tasks will have to be ensured by both parties to this agreement.

f. Facilities required for the committees to act swiftly and impartially, will have to be provided by mutual agreement.

6. Recommend establishment of communication links between S.F and L.T.T.E military area leaders which will enable them to sort out problems expeditiously, locally.

Cessation of hostilities will continue till notice of termination is given by either party. Such notice should be given at least 72 hours before termination.

Signed on 5th January 1995

V.Pirabakaran
Leader
Liberation Tigers of
Tamil Eelam

Chandrika Bandaranaike Kumaratunga
President of Sri Lanka and
Commander in Chief of the
Armed Forces

As the cessation of hostilities came into effect on the 8th of January 1995, problems arose with regards to the supervision and implementation of the truce. The ICRC informed both the government and the LTTE that they had no experienced personnel available to serve in the peace committee. An ICRC press release issued in Colombo stated the following;

"The Government of Sri Lanka and the LTTE have decided to declare a Cessation of Hostilities coming into effect from Sunday 8 January 1995. To monitor the implementation of this cessation of hostilities, it was also decided to create Peace Committees composed of representative of the LTTE, the Government of Sri Lanka and of foreign countries.

Both parties proposed the International Committee of the Red Cross (ICRC) to Chair one of these Peace committees. The Delegation of the ICRC in Sri Lanka informed the Government of Sri Lanka and the LTTE that it could not accept this proposal. The monitoring of a cessation of hostilities or cease-fire requires military expertise. Being a civilian international organisation and having a mandate centered on the implementation of International Humanitarian Law, the ICRC has not this competence and expertise. However, the ICRC informed all parties involved of its willingness to support the Peace Process and to assist the work of the Peace Committees by continuing to play its traditional role of neutral intermediary".

The Issue Of Foreign Delegates

In the meantime only four foreign delegates from three western nations (Audun Holm and Johan Gabrielson from Norway, Lt.Col. Paul Henry Horsting from Holland, Maj. Gen.C. Milner from Canada) arrived in Colombo to chair peace committees in six areas of the northeast. On the 10th January 1995 the government dispatched two of these foreign representatives to chair the peace committees in Trincomalee and Batticaloa-Amparai regions without notifying the LTTE. On the 13th January 1995 Mr. Tamilselvan sent a brief message to Mr. Balapatabendi, leader of the Sri Lanka peace delegation, registering strong protest for dispatching foreign delegates to their assignments without consulting the LTTE leadership. Since these foreign delegates were invited as neutral observers by both the parties in conflict, the LTTE desired to discuss with them before they took up their assignments as peace monitors. Mr. Tamilselvan's letter is as follows:

13.1.1995

Mr. K. Balapatabendi,
Secretary to the President

1. The LTTE considers it absolutely essential that the international chairmen discuss the cessation of hostilities with the LTTE leadership before taking up their posts. This is considered vital to ensure their role in a neutral capacity.

2. The LTTE strongly protests at the sending of the chairmen of the Batticoloa-Amparai and Trincomalee Peace Committees to their respective assignments without contact having been made with the LTTE leadership.

Signed: Mr. S. P. Tamilselvan.
Leader, Political Section
Jaffna

Mr. Balapatabendi sent the following reply to Mr. Tamilselvan.

13 January 1995

Mr. S.P.Tamilselvan
Leader/Political Section , LTTE

Have received your message of 13 January, sent through ICRC.

H.E. President has considered LTTE's views in matter, and

has arranged for discussions between LTTE leadership and Chairmen of Committees for verification of violations of Cessation of Hostilities, before latter commence their functions.

Accordingly, it has been arranged to defer commencement of work by Trincomalee and Batticaloa-Amparai committees for present.

It is hoped to enable all Chairmen of Committees, who are here at the invitation of Government, to arrive in Jaffna for discussions on Tuesday 17 January, accompanied by Government representative who would look to Chairmen's well being.

Travel details will be finalised through usual military liaison channels, and will be communicated through ICRC.

K.Balapatabendi,
Secretary to the President

Several potentially serious incidents were reported by our cadres in the Eastern districts where military personnel stationed at various check-points blocked the mobility of our fighters and warned them not to carry weapons. Unlike the North, where the army was confined to barracks, the security system of the army in the East was complex and posed several problems for the mobility of our guerilla units. In the urban areas of the Eastern Province, government troops were stationed in every nook and corner and maintaining safe distances between combatants without confrontation became almost impossible. The terms and conditions specified as modalities of the truce were inadequate and limited to deal with security issues in the Eastern Province. In addition to these problems, the government made a unilateral announcement on the 9th of January 1995 prohibiting fishing in several specified areas and also imposing a ban on night fishing. The LTTE felt that this announcement contravened the agreed modalities for the implementation of the truce which specifically stated that the security forces of the government would not cause any obstructions to legitimate and bonafide fishing. The issue of the 'specified areas' were discussed at the last round of talks and both parties agreed that fishing would not take place in the vicinity of army camps and naval bases. Therefore the new restrictions as proclaimed by the government violated the spirit of the bilateral agreement. We decided to take up these issues at the third round of direct talks.

The third round of talks took place on the 14th of January 1995 in the same venue, with the participation of the same government delegates as on the previous occasion.

At the talks, the LTTE delegation insisted that the modalities for the implementation of the truce had to be clarified and expanded to ensure the maintenance of peace and to prevent any possible violations of the cessation of hostilities. Explaining the difficulties encountered by the Tamil Tiger guerrillas in the Eastern districts, the LTTE delegates demanded guarantees from the government ensuring the freedom of mobility of their armed units. The Tigers suggested the modalities of implementation of the truce had to be clarified and specified in written form to facilitate the peace committees to monitor the bilateral agreement. The amendments to the modalities of the truce, the LTTE delegates suggested, could be worked out as a separate document or an appendix to the original declaration.

Responding to the suggestions of the LTTE delegates, Mr. Balapatabendi said that the government would consider their ideas. He asked Mr. Tamilselvan to present the problems of the Eastern Province in written form as early as possible.

On the issue of withdrawing the army camp at Pooneryn to open up a land route to the mainland, the government delegates argued that the camp could not be withdrawn for strategic and security reasons. The front defence lines of the army camp could be readjusted allowing 600 metres of distance but all the civilian passengers would be subjected to search, Mr. Balapatabendi insisted. Though our representatives explained in detail the hardships and dangers faced by our people in crossing the Kilali lagoon to make a trip to the mainland, the government delegates were not prepared to compromise on the issue.

The LTTE delegates demanded the removal of the ban on fishing in the Northeastern waters except in the vicinity of naval bases and army camps as previously agreed. The government delegates argued that the ban was imposed to check the movement of the Sea Tigers. The government representatives adopted an uncompromising attitude on certain issues which they termed as 'security concerns of the State'. Finally when the question of the removal of the economic embargo was raised Mr. Balapatabendi announced that the government would soon announce the relaxation of embargoes on some items. The LTTE delegates pointed out that several essential items, though relaxed by government notification, did not reach the Tamil population as the military personnel in Vavuniya blocked their passage. The government team promised to look into the matter.

On the 15th of January 1995, the day after the third round of talks Mr. Tamilselvan sent the following letter to Mr. Balapatabendi concerning the problems of the Eastern districts.

Political Head Office
Jaffna
15.01.1995

Mr.K. Balapatabendi,
Secretary to the President,
Sri Lanka.

As we have agreed in the last round of talks certain issues in relation to the modalities of the implementation of cessation of hostilities have to be clarified and specified in written form to facilitate the monitoring committees to supervise ceasefire effectively. This can be worked out as a separate document or as an appendix to the declaration of cessation of hostilities.

In view of the sensitive nature of the ground situation in the Eastern Province and the rigid and complex form of the security system established by the armed forces certain arrangements have to be made to ensure the freedom of mobility of our guerrilla units operating in that sector. In this matter we suggest the following:

1). For reasons of personal security, our cadres should be allowed to carry arms in the districts of Trincomalee, Batticaloa and Amparai.

2). LTTE cadres should not be subjected to checking and screening at various check points along the road ways.

3). The economic embargo imposed by the armed forces on the common people should be lifted immediately.

4). The armed forces should consider removing various road blocks and check points and desist from checking civilian passengers.

5). State sponsored colonisation schemes in Tamil areas in the Northeast should not be undertaken during the period of cessation of hostilities.

6). The armed forces should not involve in search operations and village roundups, and avoid taking ambush positions in jungle areas.

7). Fishing activity should be allowed without hindrance in the lagoons of the East.

You will appreciate that in accordance with the terms and conditions of the declaration of cessation of hostilities agreed by both parties, the Government should ensure legitimate and bonafide fishing in Northeastern waters. We agree that fishing should not take place in the vicinity of the army camps and naval bases. We urge the Government to lift the ban on night fishing and remove restrictions on limits imposed on the fishing zone.

I hope that you will give urgent consideration to these matters.
Thanking you,
Yours Sincerely

(A.S.Tamilselvan)
Leader,
Political Section
Liberation Tigers of Tamil Eelam

In a brief reply, Mr. Balapatabendi did not clarify any issues, particularly the problem of mobility of the LTTE's armed guerrilla units which posed serious difficulties for the Tigers in the East. Mr. Balapatabendi claimed that suitable arrangements had been made between field commanders of the army and the LTTE leaders. Following is the message sent by the secretary to the President.

21 January 1995

Mr. S.P. Tamilselvan
Leader/Political Section LTTE
Jaffna

Thank you for your message of 16.01.95, sent to me through the ICRC.

With regard to matters raised by you under serial 1), 2), 4), & 6), suitable arrangements have already been discussed and agreed between Area Leaders of the LTTE and the Field Commanders of the Sri Lankan Armed Forces.

Regarding item serial 3), the economic embargo is to be lifted in respect of several more items, as indicated at our last meeting. A copy of the relevant gazette notice will be sent to you as soon as it is issued.

With regard to item serial 5, it remains the position of the Government that there has been no colonization recently in the Eastern Province. There has in fact been re-settlement, both of Sinhala and Tamil families, in the areas of Andankulam, Samanthurai and Uhana, under the re-settlement programme which had commenced in 1992. The number of Tamil families thus re-settled in these areas amounts to 1060.

Regarding item serial 7), there is to be no change from prevailing practice in fishing areas for the time being. However, the Government is considering a gradual relaxation of these restrictions. The development package proposed by you is being examined, and it is hoped to provide you with an implementation programme shortly.

Signed: K. Balapatabendi
Secretary to the President

Disappointed with this 'vague and unsatisfactory' reply, Mr. Tamilselvan, in his response to Mr. Balapatabendi emphasised the importance of clarifying and elaborating the declaration of cessation of hostilities and arriving at a working arrangement. If it is not done, the formation of the peace committees and the implementation of the truce agreement 'may run into serious difficulties' cautioned Mr. Tamilselvan. The following is the text of Mr. Tamilselvan's reply.

Political Head Office
Jaffna
22nd January 1995

Mr. K. Balapatabendi
Secretary to President
Sri Lanka

Dear Mr. Balapatabendi,

Thank you for your communication dated 21st January 1995.

We are disappointed to note that your response to our queries seeking clarification on certain issues pertaining to the modalities of cessation of hostilities, particularly in the Eastern Province, is very brief, vague and unsatisfactory.

We wish to point out that no 'suitable arrangements have already been discussed and agreed', as you have claimed, between our area leaders and field commanders of the armed forces. It is because of the difficulties in reaching a suitable arrangement we have raised these issues at the last round of talks and you have suggested to state these issues in written form. In our letter dated 15.1.1995 we have specifically raised the issue of the freedom of mobility of our cadres in the Eastern Province and urged that our fighters should be allowed to carry arms for reasons of personal security and that they should not be subjected to military checking. We have also pointed out to you that the field commanders in the Eastern Province are opposed to the movement of our cadres with arms. In these circumstances we are surprised and dismayed over your claim that an agreement has been reached on this critical issue.

The item serial 3, in our letter refers to the unofficial economic embargo imposed on the Tamil civilians in several areas in the Eastern Province by the armed forces. The army, on its own, has imposed severe restrictions on various essential items including food stuffs and operating a ration system in rural areas of Trincomalee and Batticaloa, which have seriously affected the conditions of existence of our people. We have requested you to put an end to this form of economic injustice but your letter only refers to the economic blockade in the North.

The continuing restrictions and bans on the fishing zone, we wish to impress upon you, constitute a serious violation of the Declaration of Cessation of Hostilities which allows for legal and bonafide fishing activity.

You are aware that unless a working arrangement is reached on certain issues that are not elaborated and clarified in the Declaration of Cessation of Hostilities and specified in written form on mutual consent, the formation of the monitoring committees and effective implementation of the ceasefire agreement may run into serious difficulties.

Therefore, we kindly request you to give urgent and serious consideration to these matters of critical importance and clarify the Government's position in writing.

Thanking you.
With regards.
Yours Sincerely.

(S.P.Tamilselvan)
Leader
Political Section
Liberation Tigers of Tamil Eelam

A Fragile Peace

We realised in no time that the government was not prepared to compromise on any issues we raised. The military authorities wanted rigid control over the security system in the Eastern districts and was therefore opposed to the freedom of mobility of the armed LTTE guerrillas. The navy was opposed to the movement of Sea Tigers in the Northeastern coastal areas and wanted the restrictions on fishing continued. Since the government had taken an inflexible position on these matters, it was opposed to amending or expanding the original document which specified the modalities of the cessation of hostilities. Though the government delegates at the third round of peace talks agreed to modify the original truce document to deal with the security issues in the Eastern Province, they changed their position when they returned to Colombo. Mr. Balapatabendi made a specific request to Mr. Tamilselvan to write down the issues and his suggestions in relation to the situation in the East. But when Mr. Tamilselvan responded with the letter, Mr. Balapatabendi charged that the LTTE was making new demands and had therefore changed its position.

Furthermore, the LTTE wanted to meet the foreign representatives of the Peace Committees to appraise them of the ground situation in particular and the Tamil armed struggle in general. They were neutral observers invited by both the parties in conflict. Therefore the proper protocol was to make arrangements for these foreign delegates to meet the LTTE leadership, before they resume their function as Chairmen of the monitoring committees. Though the government agreed to comply with the LTTE's request, it deliberately delayed the meeting. To facilitate the foreign representatives to monitor the truce agreement effectively without bias, the LTTE wanted a comprehensive truce document specifying adequate guidelines and mechanisms of the modalities of the cessation of hostilities. We felt that the original signed document was brief and limited and therefore the Peace Committees, particularly the foreign delegates who were unfamiliar to the environment and the armed conflict, could not operate effectively in their task of maintaining peace. These matters were explained to the government delegates during the last round of talks. They did not raise any objections to our fair and reasonable requests at that time. They would have to consult the authorities in Colombo, they said. Having made their consultations, they took a different position. Mr. Balapatabendi's letter to Mr. Tamilselvan was hostile. He charged that the issues raised by Mr.Tamilselvan should have been discussed and dealt with at the time of signing the truce agreement. He cautioned that if such an attitude continued it would 'seriously impair the successful continuation of cessation of hostilities'. The full text of his letter is s follows:

26 January 1995

Mr. S.P. Tamilselvan,
Leader/Political Section,
LTTE, Jaffna.

Your communication dated 22nd January 1995 has been received and duly considered by the Government. I have now been directed to respond to it as follows: -

The Government has carefully examined the contents of your letter and is disappointed and surprised at the statement you have made which to quote from your letter reads, "....unless a working arrangement is reached on certain issues that are not elaborated and clarified in the declaration of cessation of hostilities.... and effective implementation of the ceasefire agreement may run into serious difficulties".

The written agreement entered into between the Government and the LTTE consisting the modalities of cessation of hostilities was clearly the basis on which the cessation of hostilities commenced. It was agreed by both parties very clearly that the Committees to deal with the violations of cessation of hostilities should be set up as early as possible to facilitate and solve disputes arising during the period of cessation of hostilities.

It is needless to mention that on mutual agreement 4 foreign delegates from 3 different western countries were invited to function as leaders of the Committees and they have remained in this country for over 2 weeks without being able to function, as you objected to the Committees functioning, surprisingly after a having agreed to all the details regarding the appointments of foreign delegates and to the commencement of their work in the Committees, the Committees have remained inactive.

You did not until now state that the formation and the functioning of these Committees would depend upon any other matters which may be raised during the period of the cessation of hostilities. The Committees were to be formed as soon as the cessation of hostilities came to be operative and were to function quite independently of the issues you have now raised in your recent correspondence. It is objectionable to now raise issues which were not discussed nor dealt with at the time of signing of the written agreement between our 2 sides. If this attitude continues, it would not only seriously impair the successful continuation of cessation of hostilities but also the mutual confidence and trust the Government and the LTTE have begun to create.

The Government would like to re-state the chronology of events with regard to this matter.

i) *The Government delegation discussed at the meeting on 3rd January 1995 the possibility of forming these Committees and of having delegates to chair those Committees, to which you agreed without any conditions. You even sent a list of the LTTE representatives and the Government sent you a list of their nominees.*

ii) *After the arrival of 2 of the delegates and after they took up position in Trincomalee and Batticaloa in the expectation that the Committees could start functioning together with your representatives, you suddenly informed the Government that these Committees should not function until the LTTE had discussions with the foreign delegates. Even though this was very inconvenient for all concerned but as it was a request which was made by you, the Government responded to you that they would send the foreign delegates to Jaffna to meet with you in Jaffna.*

iii) *There was a further shift in your position as noted in your letter of 16th January 1995 by you putting forward 7 demands which you stated should be satisfied before the commencement of the operation of the Committees. The Government replied to you on 21st January 1995 in their endeavour to satisfy your request.*

However, your reply dated 22nd January 1995 from which a quotation is carried above, gives an indication that you are seeking to prevent the Committees functioning under whatever circumstances.

In regard to the reply dated 21st January 1995 in respect of the matters raised by you in your letter of 16th January 1995 under serial numbers 1, 2, 4 and 6, it is stated that agreements have been reached between your Area Leaders and the Field Commanders of the Sri Lanka Armed Forces. Copies of the agreements entered between the aforesaid parties in respect of Trincomalee and Batticaloa are annexed hereto.

As stated above, the Government have arrived at solutions for most of the issues raised by you, even though they reiterated their position that the original agreements on cessation of hostilities was not contingent on any of the terms of cessation of hostilities. If any problems would arise they could be dealt with while cessation of hostilities continued and the Committees commence and continue operations.

The Government's position regarding the above matters have been clear right through the dialogue on cessation of hostilities and they hope you would reciprocate in the same manner.

The Government is also making arrangements for the foreign delegates to meet you in Jaffna on a date between 27th and 30th January. Please inform the most suitable date for you.

In regard to your contention that severe restrictions on various essential items including food stuffs have been imposed, instructions have been given to all the Field Commanders of the Armed

Forces to desist from enforcing any restrictions on the movement of essential items including food stuffs if any restrictions are in operation in that area.

In regard to lifting of the economic embargo on some of the items that were discussed at the last meeting, enclosed herewith is a further list of items on which the economic embargo has been lifted by the Government. The Gazette notice will be sent to you shortly.

Regarding the fishing areas, the Government has stated that if the cessation of hostilities was successfully carried through and there were no violations of the conditions pertaining to fishing, they would consider further relaxation of fishing areas. Nevertheless, since the cessation of hostilities was declared, our Forces have observed a large number of violations by you. Attached is a copy of the list of violations noticed during the period to date. It is also believed that you are aware of these violations and also the fact that most of those violations were resolved between our Field commanders and your Area Leaders by discussion and agreement.

Yours Sincerely.

K. Balapatabendi
Secretary to the President

Attached to the letter was a communique released by the operational headquarters of the Ministry of Defence announcing the removal of restrictions on certain items.

21 Jan 1995
OPERATIONAL HEADQUARTERS, MINISTRY OF DEFENCE
Director of Information
COMMUNIQUE 01
RESTRICTED ITEMS TO THE NORTHERN/EASTERN PROVINCES

1. *The restriction has been removed in respect of following items to the Northern Province.*
   a. *Toy guns*
   b. *Electric wire*
   c. *Electric/Electronic equipment*
   d. *Electric/ Electronic toys*
   e. *Aluminium/Aluminium ware*
   f. *Empty gunny bags*
   g. *Ball Bearings*
   h. *Motor Vehicles Spare Parts*
   i. *Printing Machines and Other Equipment used in Printing*
   j. *Gold*
   k. *Chemicals*
   l. *Batteries of all varieties except Penlight Batteries*

   J K N Jayakody
   Brigadier
   Principal Staff Officer

Mr. Tamilselvan, in his reply, rejected the accusation that the LTTE was deliberately preventing the function of the Peace Committees. Such a perception was biased and based on a total misconception of the LTTE's position, he said. He also suggested that these 'sensitive and serious matters' could be discussed and resolved at the next round of talks. Following is the full text of his letter.

Political Head Office
Jaffna
3.2.1995

Mr. K. Balapatabendi,
Secretary to the President
Colombo
Sri Lanka

Dear Mr. Balapatabendi,

Thank you for your communication dated 27ᵗʰ January 1995.

First of all we wish to clarify certain issues that have given rise to misconceptions with regard to our position on the functioning of the monitoring committees.

You are aware that foreign delegates from three different western countries were invited by both the Government of Sri Lanka and the LTTE, as the parties in conflict, to function as Chairmen of the monitoring committees. They were invited as neutral observers, by consent of both parties, to carry out a sensitive function impartially. We anticipated that the accredited foreign delegates would formally meet the representatives of both parties before they resume their functions. Such a gesture, we presumed, was vital to ensure their role in a neutral capacity and to create a better understanding of the nature of the conflict. It would have been proper protocol if the Government, which has the facilities of communication and transport, had made arrangements for such a meeting. But we were surprised to note that the Government leaders, having had a meeting with these delegates, dispatched them to take up assignments immediately in the committees at Batticaloa and Trincomalee without extending to us the courtesy of meeting them. This is why we registered our protest and demanded to meet the foreign delegates. We think our request is fair and reasonable.

In reference to this issue you have, in your letter, made an unwarranted accusation that we deliberately sought to prevent the functioning of the monitoring committees. Such a perception is biased and based on a total misconception of our position.

Furthermore, we wanted clarification and specifications from the Government on certain crucial matters with regard to modalities of cessation of hostilities before the formation of the monitoring committees so that it would help to facilitate the smooth implementation of ceasefire. When these issues were raised at the last round of talks, you suggested that these matters be forwarded in writing for consideration in Colombo. We responded to your request and listed the problems in writing, to which you state in your letter, that we have shifted our position and raising new demands.

We agree that our area leaders and the field commanders of the armed forces have met in Trincomalee and Batticaloa and worked out an interim arrangement to sort out immediate problems and disputes at local level for a short duration of time pending final decisions to be jointly made by the Government and the LTTE leadership. While we agree that some local disputes can be resolved by area commanders on both sides, as stated in the declaration of Cessation of Hostilities, we wish to state that such temporary arrangements worked out at peripheral level, cannot be considered as permanent solutions to overall issues pertaining to modalities of ceasefire, which have to be agreed upon at leadership level by both the Government and the LTTE. Therefore we insist that there are general issues requiring further discussion and clarification and an amicable settlement between both parties on such issues will help to ensure proper implementation of cessation of hostilities.

We think that it would be more appropriate that these sensitive and serious issues can be discussed and amicably resolved through direct negotiations at the next round of talks.

Thanking you.
Yours sincerely

(S.P.Tamilselvan)
Leader
Political Section
Liberation Tigers of Tamil Eelam

The LTTE team led by Mr. V. Pirabakaran, leader of the Tamil Tigers (middle), Mr. Anton Balasingham (right) and Mr. Tamilselvan (left) engaged in a discussion with the international monitoring committee.

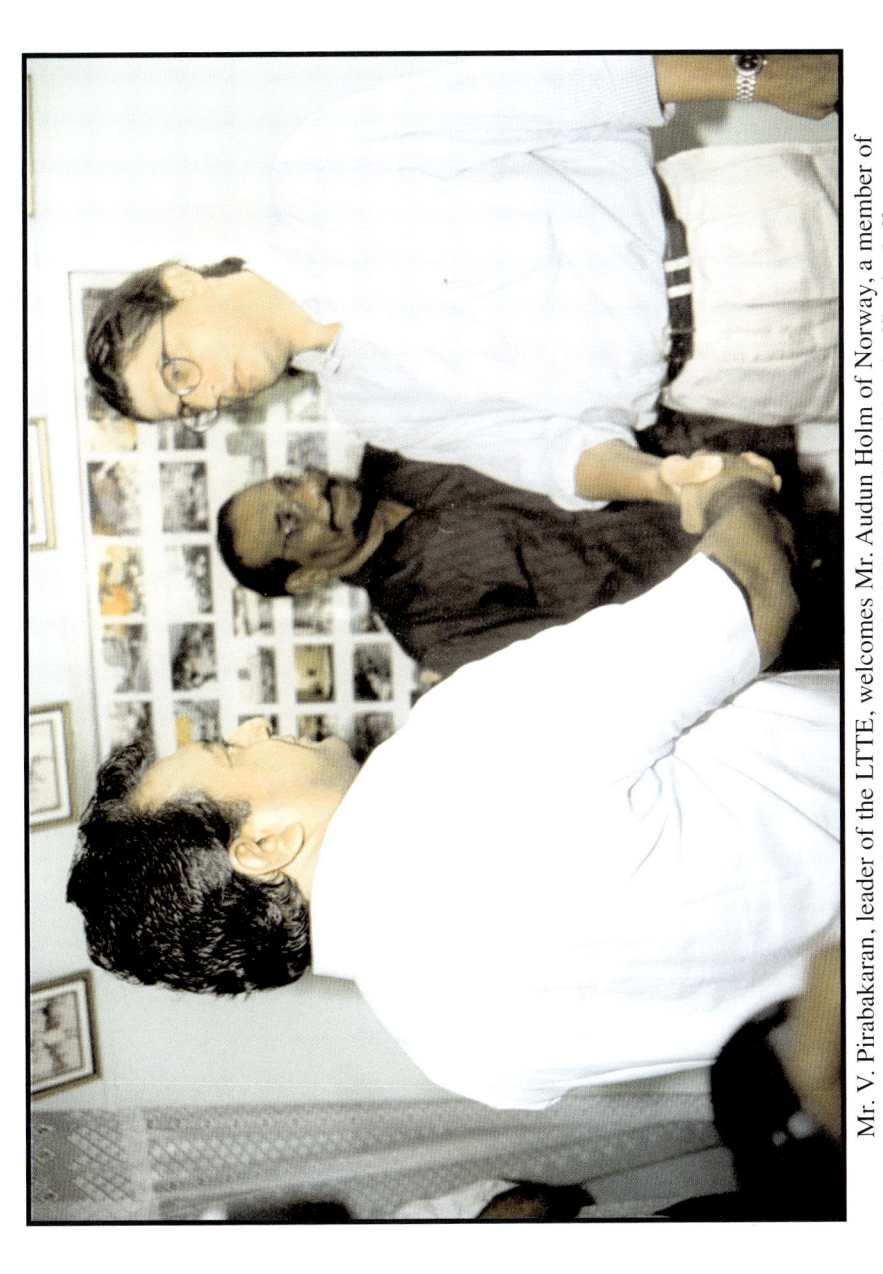

Mr. V. Pirabakaran, leader of the LTTE, welcomes Mr. Audun Holm of Norway, a member of the international monitoring committee, at the LTTE's political head office in Jaffna. Mr. Anton Balasingham is in the background.

The international monitoring committee consisting of (Left to Right) Lt. Col. Paul Henry Hosting from Netherland, Major General Clive Milner from Canada, Johan Gabrielsen and Audun Holm of Norway in discussion with the LTTE.

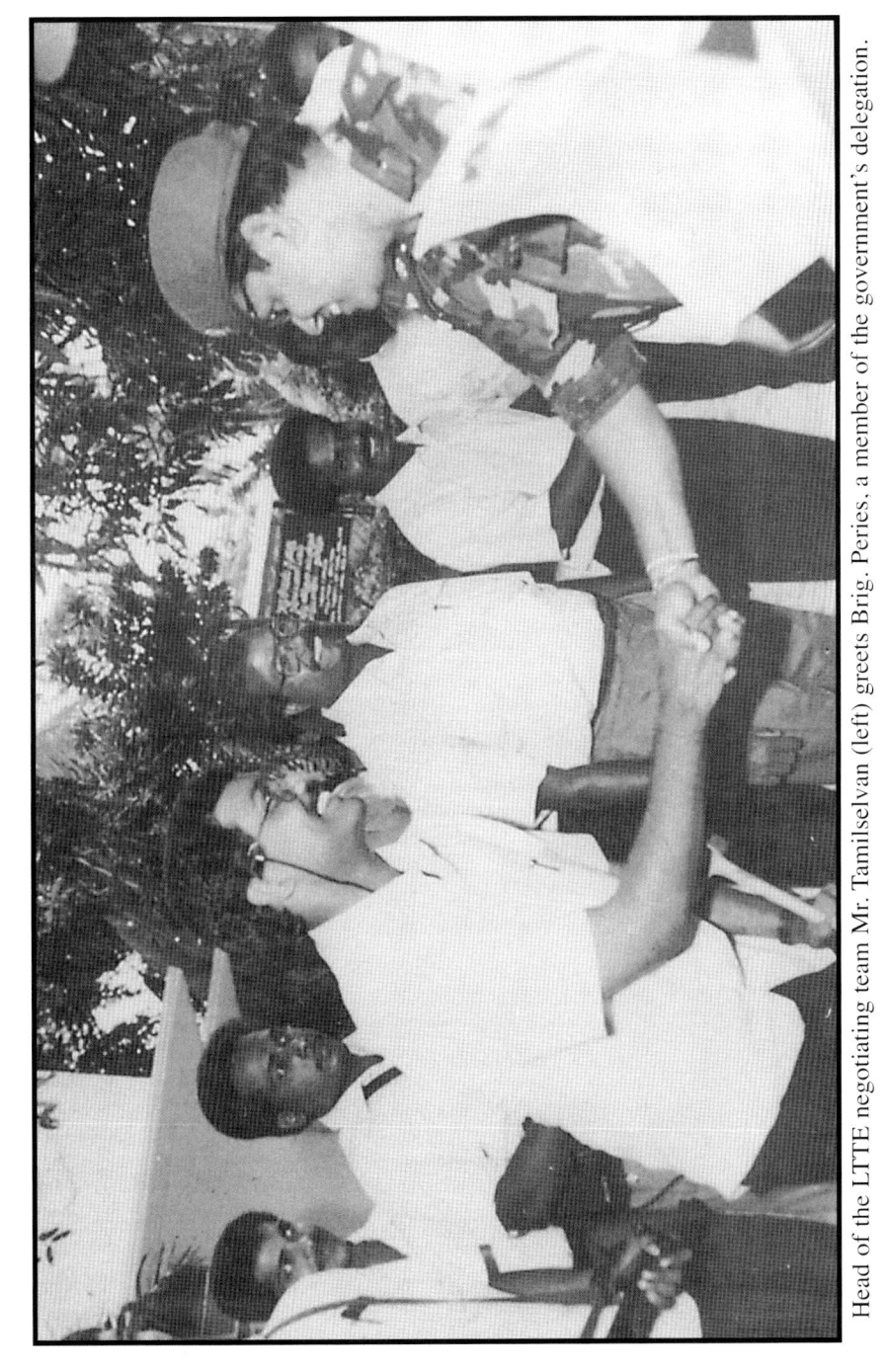

Head of the LTTE negotiating team Mr. Tamilselvan (left) greets Brig. Peries, a member of the government's delegation.

The ICRC residential delegate in Jaffna, Ms. Mary Perkins (right) along with other delegates. The ICRC played a crucial role facilitating the Jaffna talks.

LTTE Confers With Foreign Delegates

After deliberate delays, Kumaratunga's government gave the green light to the four foreign delegates to visit Jaffna to meet the LTTE representatives. The four delegates sent a brief message to the LTTE through the ICRC indicating their willingness to meet our representatives at the earliest convenience. The message read as follows:

Colombo,
31 January 1995

Dear Sirs,

Please be advised that we, the four international Chairmen of the Committees established by the Government of Sri Lanka and the LTTE to assist with the Cessation of Hostilities Agreement, feel that it is timely and appropriate that we meet with the LTTE representatives.

It is our view that introductory meetings with your representatives as well as with our respective LTTE appointed committee members will facilitate our understanding of the committee functions and be of immeasurable advantage to all parties concerned.

We are prepared to meet with your representatives at the earliest convenience.

Yours sincerely

Johan Gabrielsen / Audun Holm / Paul Horsting / Clive Milner

Mr. Tamilselvan responded by sending the following message to the foreign delegates.

Political Head Office
Jaffna
1.2.1995

The Chairmen,
Monitoring Committees
Colombo
Sri Lanka

Dear Sirs,

Thank you very much for your communication dated 31.1.1995 sent through the good offices of the ICRC.

We are pleased to inform you that we would be very glad to receive you in Jaffna on 5th February 1995. A letter to this effect has already been transmitted to Mr. Balapatabendi, Secretary to the President.

Thanking you.
Yours Sincerely.

(Mr. S.P. Tamilselvan)
Leader
Political Section
Liberation Tigers of Tamil Eelam

The foreign delegates, Audun Holm and Johan Gabrielsen form Norway, Lt. Col. Paul Henry Hosting from Netherlands and Major General Clive Milner from Canada arrived in Jaffna by a Sri Lankan military helicopter around 10 o'clock in the morning on the 5th of February 1995. They were brought to the political headquarters of the LTTE at Chundukuli from St. John's college grounds. Mr. Pirabakaran, Mr.Tamilselvan and myself received the chairmen of the monitoring committees and had a closed door meeting for nearly one hour before they met the LTTE appointed members of the peace committees. The foreign delegates were delighted over this surprise meeting with the leader and military commander of the Liberation Tigers.

Welcoming the delegates, Mr. Pirabakaran thanked the governments of Norway, Holland and Canada for sending delegates to monitor the cessation of hostilities between the Sri Lanka government and the Tamil Tigers. He pledged that the Liberation Tigers would extend support and co-operation to facilitate the effective supervision of the truce agreement by the monitoring committees.

We explained to the chairmen of the peace committees that the document specifying the modalities of the truce was very brief and limited and failed to provide adequate guidelines to several critical issues which have to be further discussed and resolved by both parties. We explained to them the nature of the ground realities in the North and East and the mounting complaints by both parties claiming violations of the truce. Unless a comprehensive document was worked out on the modalities by the consent of both parties, we argued, it would be very difficult for the peace committees to effectively monitor the cessation hostilities.

Having realised the significance of our criticism of the inadequacies of the truce document, the foreign peace monitors had a private discussion among themselves scrutinising the original declaration. Thereafter, they expressed a unanimous view that the declaration was very brief, inadequate and lacked proper guidelines to several issues. They advised us that the parties in conflict should meet without delay to discuss and formulate a comprehensive document as an annexure to the original declaration. Brigadier Peris, who accompanied the foreign delegates, endorsed the view of the chairmen of the peace committees and promised to convey the details to the government. At the end of the meeting the foreign delegates were convinced the LTTE's suggestions were fair and reasonable.

As the government deliberately delayed the formation of the peace committees, numerous incidents of violations of the cessation of hostilities were reported, particularly in the Eastern Province. Both parties continued to exchange lists of violations and accused each other.

On the 23rd of January 1995, a Sea Tiger boat carrying seven LTTE cadres was compelled to reach shore at Kalkudah, Batticaloa due to engine failure. The landing took place in the vicinity of the Kalkudah police station. The Sea Tigers were arrested and their weapons (a machine gun and rifles) walkie-talkie sets and the boat were confiscated. Later the Sea Tigers were released but their weapons and boat were kept in the custody of the security forces.

Both the parties considered this incident as a serious violation of the cessation of hostilities and protested. The LTTE argued that the sea landing was an accident. The arrest and harassment of the cadres and the confiscation of the weapons and boat were hostile acts that undermined the spirit of the truce agreement. The government portrayed the incident as the most serious violation of the truce in the Eastern Province. In a gross distortion of the facts it projected a picture of the Sea Tigers approaching the Kalkudah police station carrying heavy artillery in the boat. In response to the LTTE's strong protest over the incident Mr. Balapatabendi replied that if the peace committees were appointed these matters would have been resolved amicably. He wrote to Mr. Tamilselvan thus:

7th February 1995

Mr. S.P. Tamilselvan
Leader/Political Section,
Liberation Tigers of Tamil Eelam,
Jaffna.

Dear Mr. Tamilselvan,

It is with deep concern that I write to you about the violations that have occurred during the period of the cessation of

Hostilities, some of which are very serious.

I am sending herewith a list of violations that have been observed by the Sri Lanka forces during the period commencing from the 8th January 1995. You will observe from this list that there have been many violations, the most serious violations being those in the Eastern Province, such as the incident of the Sea Tiger boat carrying heavy artillery sailing near the Police Station of Kalkudah, in spite of the conditions laid down in the Agreement.

It is observed that the LTTE cadres are constructing new camps in Koravalikulam and Eralakulam. When the construction was earlier observed by the Sri Lanka forces, instructions were given to your Area Leaders and the camps were dismantled, but your Cadres have again started construction of these camps.

The Government also is informed that you have established a Police Station in Murunkan in the Mannar District and a base in Nadukudi in the Mannar District.

The Government is surprised to observe the most recent incident that happened in Nittambuwa at the location of the samadhi of the late Prime Minister S.W.R.D.Bandaranaike. A person named Mr. Alfred Ponnaiah Jeevaratnam was taken into custody by the local Police when he was photographing various angles of the Samadhi. He confessed that he was acting on instructions from LTTE leaders in Kilinochchi, named Senturan, Kannan and Jhan. This, the Government considers, is a serious security threat to the life of Her Excellency the President, as she visits this place frequently.

The Sri Lanka forces have also observed that there is a massive recruitment drive into the cadres of the LTTE in the Eastern Province since the Cessation of Hostilities and the government wonder whether this would lead to a possible military attack in the Eastern Province.

You will appreciate that if the Committees appointed to investigate into the violations of the Agreement of Cessation of Hostilities were in operation these matters would perhaps have been settled expeditiously and amicably, according to the terms of the

Agreement. The Government therefore strongly suggests that the Committees commence work immediately. We do not see a necessity for these Committees to withhold functioning until we arrive at an agreement on the several issues you have raised at the last meeting with the foreign delegates. We believe that the discussion on the issues raised by you and the functioning of the said Committees could go on parallely, as our Government delegation would be meeting with you for the next round of talks within a couple of days after the Committees begin to work.

I would like to hear from you very early on the above matters.

Yours sincerely,

K.Balapatabendi
Secretary to the President

Mr. Tamilselvan, in his reply, clarified and explained the issues raised by Mr. Balapatabendi. We reproduce the full text of his letter.

LTTE Political Head Office
Jaffna
13.2.1995

Mr. K. Balapatabendi
Secretary to the President,
Colombo
Sri Lanka

Dear Mr. Balapatabendi,

Thank you for your communication dated 10th February 1995.

First of all, we wish to point out to you that the LTTE is genuinely and seriously concerned about the undue delay caused in the formation of the monitoring committees with the participation of the foreign delegates. We should emphasise that the LTTE is not in any way responsible for the delay in this matter. We hold the view that it is absolutely essential for the peace committees to function as early as possible to ensure the smooth implementation of the cessation of hostilities. In this context, we feel that it is the attitude and approach of the Government that has caused this delay.

You may recall that during the last round of talks held in Jaffna on the 14.01.1995 we have discussed the limitations of the agreement of the cessation of hostilities and called for clarifications and specifications of certain issues in relation to the modalities. We have also written to you on the 15.01.1995 explaining our position on the mobility of the LTTE cadres in the Eastern Province and suggested to you that these issues can be discussed and agreed by both parties and a separate document with clarifications can be worked out as an annexure to the basic document, i.e. the declaration of Cessation of Hostilities. We made this request with the single motive of facilitating the monitoring committees to carry out their functions effectively. You will appreciate that certain crucial issues such as the mobility of armed cadres, the movement on coastal waters, fishing etc. have to be discussed and agreed by the Government and the LTTE since these matters are beyond the purview of the monitoring committees. Your negative and hostile response to our pragmatic suggestions and the deliberate delay on your part to resume the fourth round of talks to discuss these issues, have impeded the formation of the peace committees.

Furthermore, undue delay was caused by the government to enable the foreign delegates to meet the LTTE leadership. You will certainly agree that it is proper protocol to facilitate the representatives of the foreign governments to meet the leadership of the parties involved in the conflict to ensure their neutral role and to acquaint themselves with the national problem. After much persuasion you agreed to our request and we were able to meet the delegates in Jaffna last week. In our meeting with foreign delegates, we welcomed their participation and involvement in the monitoring committees and expressed our desire to activate the committees without delay. We explained to them that the Declaration of Cessation of Hostilities is a very brief document which fails to provide adequate guidelines and mechanisms of modalities to several crucial issues which have to be further discussed and resolved by the parties in conflict. The foreign delegates, having had a private discussion among themselves, expressed a consensus view that the declaration is a very brief and inadequate document without proper guidelines to several issues. They suggested that the Government and the LTTE should meet without delay to resolve the issues and work out a comprehensive document as an annexure to the agreement. It is only then, they said, the monitoring committees could function effectively. Bri.Peris, who was present at the meeting, endorsed the idea and said that he would convey the details to the Government. He also said that the fourth round of talks could be arranged as soon as possible, maybe within a week to discuss these issues.

The LTTE accepts the position of the foreign delegates and suggests that we should meet without delay and arrive at an agreement on problematic issues so that the monitoring committees could resume their functions. It is imperative that an adequate working mechanism on modalities is thrashed out by both parties before the commencement of the monitoring committees. We cannot agree with your suggestion that discussions on modalities and the functioning of the committees could proceed parallely. We believe that this matter could have been resolved amicably in time if the Government had continued discussions with the LTTE without causing undue delays. Therefore, we suggest an early meeting primarily aimed at resolving these issues and to allow the monitoring committees to resume work without further delay.

You are aware that the Declaration of Cessation of Hostilities allows for six monitoring committees to function in Jaffna, Mannar, Vavuniya, Mullaitivu, Trincomalee and Batticaloa-Amparai. But the government has opted for four committees without consulting us. We insist that there should be six monitoring committees and suggest that two more delegates each from Canada and Netherlands could be appointed without further delay.

You will appreciate that the LTTE, inspite of various provocations from the security forces, has been observing the ceasefire strictly without causing any violations to the cessation of hostilities. The list you have submitted as violations is based on misrepresentation and distortion of facts. We are enclosing herewith a separate list of violations committed by the security forces in the Eastern province. The incident you are referring as the most serious provocations has already been communicated to Col. Ratwatte. This incident took place on the 23.01.1995 at Kalkudah, Batticaloa. A Sea Tiger boat with seven of our cadres, on account of engine trouble, was compelled to land on the beach at Kalkudah This was an accident and was not in any way intended to violate the conditions of the Agreement. The boat was carrying a machine gun, not artillery as you have said. Our cadres were arrested and later released but their weapons, walkie-talkie and the boat are still held in custody. We have made several requests to regain the confiscated articles but so far this matter is not resolved. Since the incident was an accident and not a deliberate breach of the cease-fire agreement, we kindly request you to instruct the field commander of the area to hand over weapons, walkie-talkie and the boat to the LTTE. You are aware that the agreement on cessation of hostilities does not allow for confiscation of weapons, and if the weapons are not returned to us immediately, we will regard this as an unfriendly gesture that will undermine the spirit of the cease-fire agreement.

We wish to state emphatically that the LTTE is not involved in the incident at Nittambuwa. The person to whom you are referring is not a LTTE member. We are surprised and disturbed over the innuendo expressed in your letter that the LTTE poses a serious security threat to the President. This is a baseless conjecture.

Your accusation that the LTTE is constructing new camps and conducting a massive recruitment campaign in the Eastern province in preparation of a major military offensive is totally unfounded. You will agree that political cadres should enjoy the liberty of carrying out political work among our people.

It is true that we have established a police station at Murunkan in the LTTE controlled area for the civil administration which does not constitute violation of the cessation of hostilities.

We have clarified and explained issues raised by you in your letter. These matters need a thorough discussion and agreement by both parties. Therefore, we believe that negotiations should resume soon so that these crucial matters can be settled amicably.

Thanking you,
Yours sincerely

(S.P.Tamilselvan)
Leader
Political section
LTTE

Chandrika Takes Hardline Position

Between 16th February and 24th of February 1995 - in the short period of a week – the LTTE received three communications from the Kumaratunga government: two from the President and one from the Secretary to the President. Kumaratunga's letters dealt with two issues. One related to the repair and reconstruction work in Jaffna. This was a very brief letter that requested the LTTE leader to help to facilitate the technical officers who were planning to visit Jaffna to undertake repair work. The other letter, dated 20 February 1995, dealt with Chandrika's proposal to nominate a French intermediary to facilitate secret talks between the government and the LTTE, an issue which created serious controversy. The third communication was by Mr. Balapatabendi which stated that the government had unilaterally decided to open up the Pooneryn-Sangupitty Road and Elephant Pass Road for normal traffic. We publish these letters in chronological order before presenting LTTE's response and our comments.

16th January 1995.

Mr. V. Pirabhakaran
Leader
L.T.T.E
Jaffna

Dear Mr. Pirabhakaran,

I wish to inform you that the government is ready to commence some of the re-construction projects discussed by us with the

LTTE.

Work could commence immediately on:
 - the electrification of Jaffna
 - repair of the major roadways in Jaffna
 - re-construction of the Public library
 - repairs to the General hospital

Some of the other work could commence from 1st March 1995.

Our technical officers are ready to go to Jaffna any day from Monday 20 February 1995.

I shall be thankful if you could make arrangements to receive them and facilitate their work.

We shall be writing within the next two days to you about the other matters, which have been discussed between the government and the LTTE during the past few weeks.

I shall be grateful for an early reply.

Thanking you.
With kind regards.
Yours sincerely.

Chandrika Bandaranaike Kumaratunga

20th February, 1995

Mr.V.Pirabhakaran,
Leader,
L.T.T.E.
Jaffna

Dear Mr. Pirabhakaran,

The time has come for us to start a dialogue on the elements of *a political solution to the ethnic problem.*

In order to ensure to our discussions the highest degree of confidentiality and trust, I propose to you, that we use the good offices of a neutral and uncommitted person who would serve as an intermediary between our government and the LTTE to carry directly any ideas, proposals and explanations we might wish to convey to each other concerning the elements of a political solution to the ethnic problem.

This person would help us to initiate, and to progress towards the conclusion of a political settlement with the required degree of confidentiality and trust.

The person would be known only to me and a few others in the government. I am ready to make such proposals if you are ready to receive them.

The French government, which I have approached, is ready to put at our disposal for this purpose a respected French person, Mr. Francois Michel, a former Ambassador of France to Haiti and Ethiopia, now retired, on the condition that his mission would receive your formal approval and that his security would be guaranteed by both of us.

It would be well understood that this person would only act as an intermediary between us without involving French authorities in our exchanges and without making any personal input into our exchanges, so long as we desire. If either you or I do not, at any time wish the intermediary to continue to act, he shall cease to do so.

With regard to the venue of the Intermediary contacts I would, of course, meet him in Colombo, and I would like to suggest that you might wish to meet him at any place of your choice indicated by you to him.

Mr. Michel who is now in Colombo, needs to return to France for compelling personal reasons, during the period 27th February to the 14th March. In the event of an affirmative response on your part, Mr. Michel will be available to visit Jaffna with the proposal of the government prior to his departure from Colombo on the 27th of February.

In view of the paramount importance and confidentiality of this mission, it would be appropriate that you receive him personally.

With my best wishes.
Yours Sincerely.

Chandrika Bandaranaike Kumaratunga

24th February 1995

Mr. S. Tamilselvan
Leader – Political Section
L.T.T.E.
L.T.T.E. Headquarters
Jaffna.

Dear Mr. Tamilselvan,

The Government has decided to open Pooneryn Sangupiddy Road and Elephant Pass Road for normal traffic in the North.

For this purpose the Forward Defence Lines (FDL) have been moved 500 metres away from the roadway. This would facilitate the free movement of people and vehicular traffic.

This is one of a series of steps implemented by the government with the objective of alleviating the hardships suffered by the people of the North. The lifting of the embargo on all items other than items of military significance, the despatch of free food and medical items to Jaffna, the Government's offer to commence re-construction work on 20th February, which has not been responded to by the LTTE and now the opening of the two road ways for passenger and vehicular traffic form part of the government's programme to restore normalcy and ameliorate living conditions of the people of the North.

It remains now for the LTTE to do what is required of their part to facilitate free passage through these roadways.

Thanking you.
Yours Sincerely

K.Balapatabendi
Secretary to the President

We had given serious consideration to these communications before we responded, particularly to Chandrika's proposal of engaging an intermediary to initiate a political dialogue. Why did she want to engage a private person, a retired French diplomat, as a facilitator to exchange ideas? What was the reason behind her insistence on a high degree of confidentiality and secrecy? Why did she favour a backdoor channel for inter-personal communication? What could be the reason for her to opt for a third party when the direct talks between the government and the LTTE had already begun?

First of all, we felt that this mode of third party involvement was improper. A third party mediator should be neutral and acceptable to both the parties in conflict. We neither knew this French gentleman nor were we aware of his personal credentials. We were of the opinion that this French diplomat might be well acquainted to Chandrika because of her academic connections in France. In such circumstances we were sceptical as to whether he could be impartial.

Secondly, we were not opposed to the idea of a third party facilitation or mediation. We were of the opinion that we should seek third party facilitation or mediation only if the direct talks between the government and the LTTE failed. Furthermore, we preferred an international government as a third party mediator or facilitator but certainly not an individual private person. As Chandrika indicated, the person she had chosen was not a representative of the French government.

Thirdly, we did not favour a secret dialogue. Since the Tamil conflict had attracted local and international attention we preferred an open dialogue so that the ideas discussed could be transparent and subjected to public debate.

Fourthly, we felt that Chandrika could be disenchanted with the ongoing peace talks. The peace process was not progressing forward but rather bogged down at the initial stages. Constrained by purely military considerations, the government was reluctant to compromise on many issues raised by the LTTE even though it realised they were of paramount importance to the Tamil civilian masses. The LTTE could not be pressurised to engage in a political dialogue as long as these urgent existential issues were discussed and resolved. Therefore, the talks were reaching a stage of impasse. We thought that Chandrika was seeking an alternative route to overcome the stalemate in the direct negotiations.

Having carefully studied the implications of Chandrika's proposal for engaging a foreign intermediary Mr. Pirabakaran responded to her in the following manner.

LTTE Headquarters
Jaffna
25th February 1995

Hon. Chandrika Bandaranaike Kumaratunga
President of Sri Lanka
Presidential Secretariat
Colombo

Dear President,

Thank you very much for your letter dated 20th February 1995.

I do appreciate your sincere concern that the peace initiative should progress towards an amicable settlement through personal exchange of ideas, suggestions, and explanations. With this objective in view, you have suggested the good offices of a neutral intermediary.

Having given serious thought to your suggestion, we are of the opinion that the negotiating process should be conducted by accredited representatives of the Government and the LTTE. Your representatives can convey ideas and proposals for our consideration in an open dialogue. Since the talks have evoked local and international interest and concern, we feel that the issues discussed and the progress made in the political negotiations be made public.

Given our position, I wish to inform you that at this particular conjuncture we are not favourably disposed to your suggestion of a neutral intermediary for interpersonal communication. I hope you will understand.

With kind regards.

Yours sincerely,

(Mr. V.Pirabakaran)
Leader
Liberation Tigers of Tamil Eelam

On the same day, 25th February 1995, the LTTE leader dispatched another communication to President Kumaratunga as a response both to her letter of 16th February 1995 and to Mr. Balapatabendi's brief communication of 25th February 1995 addressed to Mr. Tamilselvan. Referring to the government's project of reconstruction, Mr.Pirabakaran insisted that the lifting of the embargo on fuel and other essential items, opening a land route to the Northern mainland, stabilisation of ceasefire were crucial prerequisites to embark on a massive project of reconstruction and therefore, he suggested a negotiated settlement on these issues without delay. Commenting on Mr. Balapatabendi's contention that the economic embargo on all necessary items had been lifted, the Tamil Tiger leader denounced it as a fallacious assumption. He emphasised that most of the essential items vital for the economic existence of the Tamils were still prohibited as 'military materials' and those items that had been declared lifted were blocked by the army personnel at Vavuniya. The following is the text of Mr. Pirabakaran's letter.

LTTE Headquarters
Jaffna
25th February 1995

Hon. Chandrika Bandaranaike Kumaratunga
President of Sri Lanka
Presidential Secretariat
Colombo

Dear President,

Thank you for your letter dated 16th February 1995. Please excuse the delay in our response since we have been awaiting a reply from the government to an important letter addressed to Mr. Balapatabendi, your secretary, on the 13th February 1995.

Mr. Balapatabendi, in his brief communication of 25th February 1995 addressed to Mr. Tamilselvan chose to ignore several critical issues raised by the LTTE with regard to modalities of the cessation of hostilities, the formation of monitoring committees, the resumption of peace talks and other matters and has made an extra-ordinary claim that the Government had taken all necessary steps to alleviate the hardships suffered by the people in the North.

The Government is fully aware of the position of the LTTE with regard to the opening up of a passage between the Jaffna peninsula and the Northern mainland. Ignoring our view on this crucial issue, Mr. Balapatabendi has made a unilateral announcement, re-stating the government's old position, that the pathways (Pooneryn and Elephant Pass) have been opened to the public. This pronouncement might help to propagate a disinformation campaign but will not in anyway serve to promote the peace process. Needless to say we are deeply disappointed. Such unilateral decisions demonstrate the fact that your Government has given primacy to the strategic interests of the occupational army over and above the urgent needs of the Tamil civilian masses.

You are fully aware that the economic embargo is not fully lifted. Several essential items, i.e. petrol, diesel, motor vehicles, vehicle spare parts, batteries, fertilisers etc, which are vital for the social and economic life of our people are still banned under the prohibited category of 'military materials'. Furthermore, even the relaxed items are not reaching the public because of the self-imposed restrictions by the army at Vavuniya. This is the reality of the situation. Our people in the North are fully aware of this reality. Yet, Mr. Balapatabendi writes to inform us that the embargo on all necessary items has been lifted. This is far from the truth. Such fallacious assumptions contradicting the reality of the situation might serve as a tool for propaganda but will not alleviate the suffering of our people nor help to further the interest of peace.

What perturbs us more is the apparent lack of interest on the part of the Government to take constructive steps to transform the current cessation of armed hostilities into a stable, full-fledged cease-fire. We have addressed several letters to this effect calling for detailed discussions and clarification of several issues pertaining to modalities of cease-fire, but to our disappointment the Government has not responded positively. Such a disinterested attitude on the part of the government has caused undue delay in the formation of monitoring committees, to be chaired by foreign delegates, which are crucial for the stabilisation of the conditions of cease-fire. This is a serious matter and the failure on the part of the government to resolve this issue will seriously undermine the conditions of peace.

You will appreciate that the lifting of the embargo on fuel and other essential items, the opening of a passage to Jaffna, the stabilisation of the conditions of cease-fire, are of fundamental importance to undertake major programmes of reconstruction and development of the North. Therefore, we call upon the Government to seek a negotiated settlement to these critical matters with the LTTE so that it would facilitate the practical implementation of major reconstruction projects in the war affected areas. In this context, we wish to point out to you that our delegation, at the last round of talks, had suggested the formation of an appropriate authority comprising Government representatives and the LTTE be constituted with adequate authority to plan and implement all reconstruction projects. This suggestion was accepted by the Government delegates. Therefore, we urge the government to act according to the agreement made at the peace negotiations which will help the speedy and smooth implementation of any reconstruction projects.

We hope you will give earnest and serious consideration to our suggestions.
Thanking you.
With kind regards.
Yours sincerely,

(V.Pirabakaran)
Leader
Liberation Tigers of Tamil Eelam

Controversy Over French Intermediary

Controversy arose in Colombo political circles when the letters of exchange between President Kumaratunga and the LTTE leader on the issue of French intermediary were leaked to the press. We were puzzled as to why a secret communication treated with top level confidentiality was divulged to the media by government sources. The real objective behind the disclosure we later realised, was to unleash a false propaganda campaign claiming that the LTTE was opposed to international third party mediation. To counter this disinformation campaign and to present the true facts we decided to release the letters of exchange to the local media. Tamil translated versions of the texts of the letters of exchange on the French intermediary issue appeared in the Jaffna newspapers and were also broadcast over the Voice of Tigers radio.

On the 6th of March 1995, I called a press conference in Jaffna and explained in detail as to why Chandrika's proposal was unacceptable to the LTTE. The French intermediary, though recommended by the French government, was a private individual retired from diplomatic service and was not an accredited representative of the French government, I clarified. The French gentleman concerned could be an acquaintance of the President but unknown to the LTTE and therefore could not function as an impartial intermediary. I emphasised that the LTTE was not opposed to international third party facilitation or mediation. We would seek such an option in the event that direct talks between the government and the LTTE failed, I explained.

The political committee of the LTTE in Jaffna issued a statement in Tamil on the 7th of March, which contained the translated texts of the letters of exchange and also a version of my press interview. The LTTE's International Secretariat in London translated again into English the Tamil version of the statement by the political committee and released it as a press statement. This whole process involved the original English texts of the letters being translated into Tamil, and again the Tamil version being translated into English, and therefore discrepancies and discordance between the original text and the translated version appeared.

President Kumaratunga in her letter to Mr. Pirabakaran dated 9th March quoted a paragraph from the London press release to indicate the textual variation between the original communication and the press statement.

Without realising that the discrepancy was the result of textual translation, she accused the political committee of the LTTE of speculating about the contents of letters and misconstruction of facts. The LTTE's characterisation of the French diplomat as a private person and a friend of hers were unfounded, she said. The intermediary was selected by the French government and enjoyed French patronage, she argued.

Commenting on the day to day urgent problems of the Tamils for which the LTTE demanded immediate resolution before the dialogue on political issues, Chandrika categorically stated that granting those requests would result in serious military repercussions, since they were issues of national security. The tone and content of the letter was accusative and uncompromising. Rejecting the LTTE's position of the stage by stage approach, the letters reasserted the government's stand that talks on day to day problems and the political issues should be conducted simultaneously. In conclusion, Chandrika proposed that the talks on a political settlement should commence between 2nd and 10th April 1995. This is the text of Chandrika's letter.

9th March 1995

Mr. V. Pirabhakaran,
Leader,
L.T.T.E
Jaffna.

Dear Mr. Pirabhakaran,

I gather from a press release issued by the Political Committee of the International Secretariat of the LTTE on 7th March that there are two major issues regarding the LTTE's dialogue with the Government.

1. According to the communiqué, your letter to me dated 25th February 1995 said: "it is our desire that the talks between the Liberation Tigers and the Sri Lankan Government should be open and not secret. In a situation where the international community as well as our people are closely watching the *progress of our talks with the Government, we do not see that it would be proper or advisable for us to exchange views in secret through a private individual. We have examined with care the questions that you have raised in your letter. We desire that the talks should take place between representatives appo0inted by you on behalf of the Sri Lanka government and those appointed by us. Your representatives can make clear your views and our representatives can do the same on our behalf. It is talks on this basis between the two sides that will be fruitful. Our problems have today attracted international attention. The international community and our people are today giving their close attention to the Tamil ethnic question. Our people wish and expect to be kept informed of the talks between the two sides and its progress. In this situation, it will not be proper for me to exchange views with you through a private individual in secret." I have received only one letter from you dated 25th February 1995, and the above stated paragraph from the communiqué does not appear in the said letter.*

We regret to note that the political committee of the LTTE is obviously not aware of the contents of your letter dated 25th February and are speculating on its contents. This has led to a misconstruction of the facts contained in the only letter written by you to me on the said date.

I would like to specifically draw your attention to the fact that my letter to you dated 20th February 1995 states thus: "the French Government, which I have approached, is ready to put at our disposal for this purpose, a respected French person..... a former Ambassador of France .... On the condition that his mission would receive your formal approval and that his security would be guaranteed by both of us. It would be well understood that this person would only act as an intermediary between us without involving the French authorities in our exchanges...."

It was thus made clear that the person proposed would undertake this mission under the patronage of the French Government and that in fact he was selected by the French government for our joint approval. He would be acting according to the wishes of the Government and the LTTE, without any interference by the French Government in the exchanges between us.

The statement that the intermediary by the French government is a private individual and that he was a close friend of mine is wholly unfounded. In fact he was not known to me at all. He was selected by the French Government and I met him for the first time when he arrived in Colombo. In these circumstances the Government regrets that the LTTE appears to have misconstrued the facts on the basis of a non-existent letter.

2. The communique also says that the LTTE has been ready for talks but the said letter of the LTTE dated 25th February 1995 does not anywhere state what 'talks' you mean.

Despite my requests to you for fixing an early date for political talks, you have so far not acceded to that request. Instead you have laid down certain pre-conditions for the resumption of the talks which had started on rehabilitation and reconstruction. These conditions are as follows:
- *(i) the removal of the Pooneryn army camp.*
- *(ii) total lifting of the ban on fishing in the Northern Eastern sea.*
- *(iii) the possibility of free movement for armed LTTE cadres in the Eastern Province.*
- *(iv) the total lifting of the embargo on goods.*

All of these demands could have serious military repercussions if granted outside the framework of an established and durable peace. In the case of all these requests the Government has made the maximum possible concessions without compromising national security.

The government has also insistently stated that negotiations to these matters need not delay the commencement of political talks since the two could proceed parallely. This continues to be the position of my Government. The government proposal is that instead of trying to solve issues one by one, simultaneously talks should be held concerning the day to day problems of the people of the North and finding a political settlement to the ethnic problem.

I appreciate the suggestion made in your letter dated 25th February 1995 that 'the negotiating process should be conducted by the accredited representatives of the Government *and the LTTE.'*

I accept this suggestion and now propose that the said talks regarding the political settlement of the ethnic problem should commence on any dates between 2nd to 10th April. We would send our delegation to Jaffna for a two day period initially. Our package of proposals for a political settlement would be sent to you in advance.

I shall be grateful for an early reply.
With kind regards.

Yours Sincerely,

Chandrika Bandaranaike Kumaratunga

The LTTE was well aware that the government wanted to protect and promote the strategic interests of the military when it persistently and stubbornly refused to consider the requests made by the Tigers to alleviate the suffering of the Tamil people. Yet it was the first time that President Kumaratunga admitted openly, without any evasions and ambiguities, that granting the LTTE's request would trigger serious military implications and that it would amount to compromising 'national security'. It was a plain and outright rejection of the LTTE's position of stage by stage progressive movement of talks from the existential to the political sphere. In efffect the Government and the military establishment were not favourably disposed to the LTTE's thesis that normalisation of civilian life was a pre-requisite to political dialogue. Since Kumaratunga's government had clearly defined its stand, the Liberation Tigers were compelled to review their position and make a decision. In our evaluation of the entire range of issues, we felt that the government was not sincere in its declared objective of peace, harmony and ethnic reconciliation but rather adopted a confrontationist approach.

First of all, the economic embargo continued rigidly though the government issued periodic gazette notifications lifting the ban on several items. Fuel, fertilisers and cement were permanently banned as 'war materials'. But none of the other items reached the people even though we made repeated pleas in direct talks and in several written communications. Apart from the LTTE, the Government Agents of Tamil districts, Citizen's Committees, Confederations of People's Organisations, University Teacher's Association, inter-religious bodies made persistent and repeated appeals to President Kumaratunga and to the international human rights organisations registering strong protests that essential items, though allowed by the government, did not reach the Tamil areas. There seemed to be a tactical understanding between the Defence Ministry and the military establishment to ensure that the permitted items did not reach the Tamil people. The government was fully aware of the tragic situation faced by our people. Instead of remedying the critical situation, Kumaratunga government launched an effective international campaign that it had lifted the economic ban totally and granted the Tamils all possible concessions.

Secondly, the government deliberately ignored our call for a stable, permanent ceasefire, effectively supervised by an international monitoring committee. Instead the government favoured a loosely conceptualised temporary cessation of hostilities. Our persistent call to formulate, with mutual consent, a well-defined comprehensive framework of modalities was deliberately rejected by the government. This attitude led us to question the intentions of the government.

Thirdly, Kumaratunga's government wanted to establish total maritime supremacy in the Northeastern territorial waters with the intention of paralysing the movement of the Sea Tigers. The ban on fishing was intended for that purpose. Though the government was fully aware of the immense suffering experienced by the Tamil fishing community, it was not prepared to lift the ban on fishing.

Fourthly, the government was opposed to the free mobility of our armed cadres in the Eastern Province and consistently rejected our request to work out an amicable arrangement. We signed the Declaration of Cessation of Hostilities on the basis of the pledge given by the government delegation that the issue would be discussed and suitable arrangements would be worked out to ease the problems of the East. But later, the government refused to discuss the issue. We had several armed combat units in the Eastern districts involved in mobile guerrilla operations before the truce. The absence of any modalities or guidelines in the declaration of cessation of hostilities created grave problems for the movement of our armed cadres. We were desperate to prevent clashes that would amount to serious violations of the truce. But the government deliberately allowed a tense and unstable situation in the East and repeatedly complained of truce violations by the LTTE.

Fifthly, the government refused to withdraw the army camp at Pooneryn for specific strategic reasons. We knew very well that the Sri Lankan military under the U.N.P established the army camp at Pooneryn in 1992 with the motive of encircling the peninsula as part of an overall strategy of invading Jaffna. The plan was later postponed in favour of army operations to secure total military domination of the Eastern Province before the Jaffna offensive. We had grave concerns that Chandrika's administration would revive this military plan and launch a major offensive operation against Jaffna. The obstinate refusal on the part of the government to withdraw the army camp at Pooneryn reinforced our suspicions.

Finally, and most importantly, we knew that Kumaratunga's government was involved in a grand project of expanding and modernising the armed forces while engaging in a discourse of peace with the Tamil Tigers. During the period of the peace talks the government had purchased new supersonic combat aircraft, helicopter gunships, gunboats, tanks, armoured vehicles, heavy artillery pieces and other war materials. During this period the government had enlisted several thousand new recruits into the armed forces. This massive project of modernising and expanding the armed forces under the façade of a peacemaking process and the non-compromising and inflexible attitude shown by the government generated serious apprehensions regarding the real motives of Kumaratunga's regime. Mr. Pirabakaran was convinced that the government was insincere and buying time under the cover of peace talks to prepare for a major invasion of the Jaffna peninsula. He felt that the government was taking us for a ride in a futile political exercise and that time was running out for us.

LTTE Issues Deadline

After carefully considering all the implications, the LTTE leadership decided to issue a deadline for the government to reconsider its position. Accordingly Mr. Pirabakaran wrote the following letter to President Kumaratunga detailing the LTTE's frustrations and specifying a deadline for the possible termination of talks.

LTTE Headquarters
Jaffna
16.3.1995

Hon. Chandrika Bandaranaike Kumaratunga
President of Sri Lanka
Colombo.
Dear President,

Thank you for your letter dated 9th March 1995.

The first part of your letter refers to certain discrepancies in the contents of a press release issued by the International Secretariat of the LTTE with regard to your suggestion of a neutral intermediary. I think it would be appropriate to consider my personal communication to you as the point of reference on this matter.

You will appreciate that from the outset we have been emphasising the creation of genuine conditions of peace and restoration of normal civilian life as essential pre-requisites for the promotion of peace negotiations. We have taken up this position for specific reasons.

We are of the opinion that a durable condition of peace effected by a stable ceasefire is absolutely essential to embark on a difficult, *time consuming negotiating process aimed at resolving the highly complex ethnic conflict. You would have observed that in the past, political negotiations collapsed as a consequence of unstable ceasefires, the breaches of which led to resumption of armed conflict. I regret to say that your Government has not taken our view seriously on this critical issue. This is very evident in the approach of your government by emphasising the category of cessation of hostilities which means a temporary suspension of armed hostilities, rather than utilising the full meaning of the concept of ceasefire. Furthermore, the disinterested disregard on the part of the Government to our continuous plea to work out a comprehensive mechanism pertaining to modalities of ceasefire demonstrates the fact that your government shows little or no concern for the stabilisation of the conditions of peace.*

You are certainly aware that conditions of normal civilian life have been seriously disrupted in the Northeast as a direct consequence of the repressive racist policies of the previous administration, which sought a ruthless military approach to resolve the Tamil national question. Our people have been subjected to enormous suffering and hardship as a result of various bans, prohibitions and restrictions that were imposed on their social and economic existence primarily for the sake of facilitating military occupation and domination of the Tamil homeland. The LTTE as well as the Tamil people, entertained a hope that your new Government, which assumed power with the mandate for peace, would alleviate these hardships and create a congenial atmosphere of peace and normalcy. Based on this hope we have been pleading that the initial stages of the peace negotiations should give primacy to, what we have characterised as, urgent and immediate issues confronting the Tamil people. At the peace talks we have specified these issues, which are of paramount importance to the day to day existence of our people, and called upon the Government to redress these grievances. We have consistently emphasised that these are not demands of the LTTE, but rather urgent humanitarian needs of an aggrieved people and that these issues have to be resolved to restore normal conditions of civilian life in the war affected areas. Though, at the initial stages of the talks, your government pledged to 'alleviate the hardships of daily life presently experienced by the people', later, as the negotiations proceeded we could notice a deliberate attempt to circumvent these issues under the argument that political issues underlying the ethnic conflict should be given primacy. We have referred to this matter in our previous communications and attributed this reluctance to resolve the urgent and immediate issues to the Government's desire to placate the military hierarchy and pointed out that this approach of giving primacy to the strategic interests of the military over and above the existential concerns of a civilian population, would pose a serious threat to the peace process.

Our perception on this critical issue and our apprehension about the military designs are confirmed by your latest letter when you say that the granting of some of the 'demands' put forward by the LTTE could spark off 'serious military repercussions'. The issues we have raised as urgent needs of the people, particularly the facilitating of a passage to Jaffna by removing Pooneryn army camp, lifting the economic embargo on essential items, withdrawing the ban on fishing, are, in your view, problems of national security which cannot be compromised. In otherwords, you are attempting to legitimise the constraints and sanctions imposed by the military on the social and economic life of the Tamil people as essential requirements for the maintenance of 'national security'.

We are deeply perturbed and dismayed over your position on this critical matter which deeply affects our people. This position, based on a mistaken conception, that reduces the rights and liberties of a community of people to potential threats to national security, presupposes not only pure militarism but also hidden elements of chauvinism.

The refusal to resolve the most urgent issues that beset our people as uncompromising security issues indicates the fact that your Government is determined to perpetrate the military and economic coercions on the Tamils as bargaining cards to seek political gains at the negotiating table. It is because of this view that you are insisting that these issues should be resolved within the framework of an overall political settlement. We cannot agree to this position. The immediate day to day problems that confront our people are not political issues arising from ethnic contradictions, but rather problems engineered by the military with clearly defined strategic objectives. We are of the opinion that these bans, restrictions and prohibitions are repressive military actions instituted by the previous Government which are unfair and inhuman and have to be resolved on humanitarian grounds; on grounds of building genuine peace and goodwill between the estranged nations.

In our several communications addressed to you during the last six months and during the peace negotiations we have been consistently reiterating the urgency of resolving the immediate day to day problems of our people. Our insistence on these issues should not be misconstrued as attempts to bypass discussions on fundamental political issues underlying the ethnic conflict. We have never refused to discuss political issues. We have even gone to the extent of suggesting a suitable political framework that could satisfy the national aspirations of our people. The underlying cause for the current impasse in the peace process has nothing to do with the resumption of the political dialogue but rather the reluctance on the part of your government to deal with the immediate and urgent issues on grounds of 'military repercussions'.

If your government continues to adopt this hardline attitude on issues that need urgent resolution and which could be resolved without difficulty if there is a genuine will, we have grounds to suspect whether your Government would be able to resolve the most complex and difficult issue i.e. the national conflict. Therefore, we urge you once again to reconsider your decision for the cause of peace. If a favourable response is not received from you before the 28th March 1995, we will be compelled to make a painful decision as to whether to continue with the peace process or not.

Anticipating an early reply.
With regards.
Yours Sincerely

(V.Pirabakaran)
Leader
Liberation Tigers of Tamil Eelam

President Kumaratunga must have been taken aback by Mr. Pirabakaran's letter stipulating a deadline for the government to reconsider its position. There was no immediate response from Chandrika. Instead, Mr. Chandrananda De Silva, the Secretary of Defence, sent a message to Mr.Pirabakaran through the Government Agent of Jaffna seeking permission from the LTTE for the peace delegation to visit Jaffna on 21st March 1995. Mr. Ponnambalam, the Jaffna Government Agent, sent a brief letter in Tamil to Mr. Pirabakaran conveying a telephone message from the Secretary of Defence. Mr. Tamilselvan sent the following reply to the Secretary of Defence:

LTTE Political
Headquarters
Jaffna
21.3.1995

Mr. Chandrananda De Silva
Secretary of Defence
Colombo.

Dear Sir,

Thank you very much for your communication of 20.3.1995 addressed to our leader Mr. V. Pirabakaran.

I am instructed by the leadership to convey to you that we have very clearly stated our position in the latest letter sent by Mr.Pirabakaran to the President on 16.3.1995. We expect the Government to make positive decisions on the urgent issues affecting our people, as we have already explained. We will very much appreciate if these decisions are announced publicly and action taken to implement them immediately.

Yours Sincerely.

(S.P.Tamilselvan)
Leader
Political Section
Liberation Tigers of Tamil Eelam

On the 21st of March 1995, Chandrika Kumaratunga dispatched a brief letter to Mr. Pirabakaran stating that there was misunderstanding on several issues and that further dialogue would help to make 'positive decisions'. She informed us that the government's peace delegation, apart from Mr. Balapatabendi, would include Rt. Rev. Bishop Kenneth Fernando, Dr. Jayadeva Uyangoda and Mr. C. Abeysekara. The following is the text of that communication.

21st March, 1995

Mr. V. Pirabakaran,
Leader, L.T.T.E.,
L.T.T.E., Headquarters
Jaffna.

Dear Mr. Pirabakaran,

With reference to your letter dated 16.03.1995.

It appears that there is misunderstanding on several issues.

I believe that direct dialogue would help arrive at positive decisions. I suggest therefore that a delegation compromising of the following persons meets your delegation as there are some special issues that I would like them to discuss with you personally. They could visit Jaffna on any of the following days, 23rd, 24th, 25th March.

Rt. Rev. Bishop Kenneth Fernando,
Mr. K. Balapatabendi,
Dr. Jayadeva Uyangoda,
Mr. C. Abeysekara.

Yours Sincerely,

President

We were disappointed that the President did not take our deadline seriously. Instead, she brushed it off as a triviality arising out of misunderstanding. From one of her later communications we realised that she was annoyed with our stipulation of a deadline which she categorised as an 'ultimatum'. She presumed that a rebel movement did not have the legitimacy to issue an 'ultimatum' to a constitutionally constituted government and such an 'ultimatum' should not be entertained. It was this position which finally jeopardised the peace talks. Mr. Pirabakaran in his reply to Kumaratunga, reasserted the deadline and demanded decisions and their implementations without delay. His letter stated:

LTTE Headquarters
Jaffna
22.3.1995

Hon. Chandrika Bandaranaike Kumaratunga
President of Sri Lanka
Presidential Secretariat
Colombo.

Dear President,

Thank you for your communication of 21st March 1995.

In our letter addressed to you on 16.3.1995, we have clarified and explained our perception as well as our position with regard to the current peace negotiations.

We sincerely feel that the peace process will not serve any meaningful purpose if it is not aimed at consolidating the conditions of peace and resolving the most urgent and immediate problems faced by the Tamil people. It is in this context we urged you to reconsider your position and take positive decisions before the 28th March 1995.

Since we have made our position very clear I do not think a further dialogue is necessary to clarify what you call 'misunderstanding on several issues'. We have discussed these issues in direct dialogue and in letters of exchange for the last six months. We are of the opinion that the time has come for you, as the Head of State, to make positive decisions and to ensure such decisions are implemented without delay. Therefore, I should say that the future of the peace process rests entirely in your hands.

Thanking you.

Yours Sincerely.

(V.Pirabakaran)
Leader
Liberation Tigers of Tamil Eelam

On the 24th of March 1995, we received two communications from Chandrika. The first one dealt with a different issue entirely, alleging groups of persons purporting to be government representatives or emissaries conveying misinformation to the LTTE to sabotage the peace process. The message requested the LTTE leader not to entertain such persons without her intimation. The letter stated:

24th March 1995

Mr. V.Pirabhakaran,
L.T.T.E. Leader, Jaffna.

Dear Mr. Pirabhakaran,

I shall be writing to you in reply to your letters dated 16th March 1995 and 22nd March 1995, later on today.

In the meantime, I have had information that various groups of persons are attempting to sabotage the peace process undertaken by us with you for varying reasons, some political and others personal. This is being done by conveying misinformation to you, designed to confuse the relationship between us.

I wish to clearly state that anyone who would come to discuss with you and the LTTE purporting to be our government representatives/emissaries would be by prior intimation to you. Anyone else, however close they may claim to be to me or to the government and purporting to represent me, without any such intimation by me, should be considered as an unauthorised person.

Yours Sincerely

**Chandrika Bandaranaike Kumaratunga
President**

We were rather puzzled as to whom the President was referring to in the letter as unauthorised emissaries. During the period of peace talks several groups of persons from the South visited Jaffna and met the LTTE leaders. Most of them were journalists, political analysts, diplomats, Christian clergymen and other well wishers concerned with peace and conflict resolution. None of them claimed to be representatives or emissaries of the government or the President. Among the varieties of individuals and groups, we could identify only two persons who visited Jaffna on study tours claiming to be friends of Chandrika: one was Vasantha-Raja, Chairman of the National Television Network, Rupavahini and the other was Victor Ivan, the editor of Ravaya. Neither of them presented himself as a representative or emissary of the government or the President. Both expressed sincere concern that the talks should succeed.

Vasantha-Raja met Tamilselvan and me and had a lengthy discussion with us. His main mission at that time was to explore the possibility of setting up a television studio in Jaffna to transmit programmes to the Sinhalese people about the events and developments in the North. He also wanted to do programmes intimating the social, cultural and political life of the Sinhala people to the Northern Tamils. His objective was to create a better understanding between the North and the South. We readily agreed to his project. But we learnt later that Chandrika rejected his proposal.

The LTTE had a great regard for Victor Ivan. He was a progressive journalist with a revolutionary past. He came to Jaffna with a team of writers. I met him in Jaffna when the talks had reached a stalemate. He enquired as to whether or not the LTTE would compromise on its demands. I explained in length that the LTTE was seeking redress from various modes of repressive restrictions that severely affected the social and economic life of the people. I complained that there was growing mutual distrust and the peace process was in danger as a consequence of the government's militaristic calculations. At that time Victor was not convinced that Chandrika's administration had a secret strategic agenda of invading the North. Victor was one of the several radical thinkers who championed the cause of Chandrika at the initial stages but later became disillusioned with her authoritarian and militaristic approach. We ignored her caution about the pretending emissaries.

In her second communication on the evening of the same day (24th March 1995) President Kumaratunga asserted that her government would not entertain 'any ultimatum issued by the LTTE'. Describing it as an 'unfriendly action' that could 'jeopardise the peace process', she argued that entering into a peace dialogue with an armed organisation without the pre-condition of laying down arms was a privilege accorded to the LTTE. Having made these unfriendly remarks and reasserted the old position that the maximum had been done to alleviate the suffering of the Tamil people, Chandrika declared that her government had made positive decisions to lift the ban on fuel and fishing. She also pledged that these decisions would be implemented not later than the Tamil-Sinhala New Year (14th April 1995). The full text of her letter reads:

24th March 1995

Mr. V. Pirabhakaran.
LTTE Leader,
LTTE Headquarters,
Jaffna.

Dear Mr. Pirabhakaran,

I acknowledge your letters dated 16th March and 22nd March with thanks.

Before I commence replying to the issues contained there in, I take this opportunity to express my gratitude and that of my government to you personally and to the LTTE, for having released 16 prisoners, last Saturday. We appreciate your decision as an expression of your desire to continue the dialogue with our government.

As for the issues raised by you, I would firstly like to state that the government cannot entertain any ultimatums issued by the LTTE. I regret to state that we perceive this as an unfriendly action on your part, which could jeopardise the peace process.

You are aware that the PA government has adopted many actions which other governments might have hesitated to adopt, as part of the peace process, with the objective of finding a lasting solution to the ethnic question.

1. *Democratically established governments usually demand at least a symbolic laying down of arms, before entering in any dialogue with armed organisations. Examples abound in this respect, all over the world. Our government not only refrained from raising this issue but agreed to come to your headquarters in Jaffna.*
2. *We have also agreed to the limited movements of LTTE cadres, carrying arms, in the Eastern Province during the cessation of hostilities; this is another privilege never accorded by governments in similar circumstances.*

In addition to this we have,

3. *Lifted the embargo on most goods.*
4. *Implemented a cessation of hostilities.*
5. *Partially lifted the ban on fishing.*
6. *Decided to open alternative routes to Jaffna.*

We regret to state that due to administrative and other impediments, even goods on which the embargo had been lifted were not reaching the North in sufficient quantities. When we were informed of this situation we took immediate action by opening an additional checkpoint at Poonewa and to remove all other obstacles that hindered the flow of goods to North. May I mention here that our anxiety to open Elephant Pass and Sangupiddy routes was in order to facilitate the free flow of goods.

All these were conscious decisions taken by me and our government, not because we were unfamiliar with the manner and methods of negotiations between a government and organisations such as yours, but because we sincerely wanted to build anew the mutual trust, confidence and fraternity between the government, the Tamil people and the LTTE which was so badly ruptured through the years and especially during the tenure of the last UNP government.

While reiterating what I have stated above that we find your ultimatum unacceptable, I wish to inform you that the 3 issues raised in your letter of 16th march and on several occasions previously, have been under continuous consideration by us.

We have arrived at positive decisions on these issues. However, the implementation of these decisions required discussions with regard to certain practical details. Furthermore, we also wished to avoid the appearance of unilateral action, mindful of your concern for joint decision making in regard to such matters. Also, we thought it would be good to announce these decisions with the Sinhala Tamil New Year day in view. This is why we proposed that we meet and discuss all this with you this week, before the political talks which we proposed should commence between 2-10 April. But you have refused to dialogue with us both your above mentioned letters.

With regard to the 3 issues raised on page 3 of your letter of 16th March, we have arrived at the following decisions: -

  a. Re "the withdrawing of the fishing ban".

   The removal of all restrictions on fishing, except within a 2 mile distance from each Security Forces camp located by the shore.

    b. Re "lifting the economic embargo on essential items"

    The embargo on fuel would be lifted. All other essential items have already been released from the embargo.

    c. Re "the removal of Poonaryn Camp"

    The camp has already been shifted 600 metres away from the road. This is consistent with the LTTE's request to the UNP government through the UNHCR in 1993.

As decided earlier by us, we intend to commence the implementation of these decisions not later than the Sinhala and Tamil New Year 1995. However, we still feel that implementation could be made more effective through consultation between us.

In conclusion, may I call your attention to the encouraging statement in your first letter to me dated 2nd September 1994. "We wish to reiterate that we are prepared for ceasefire and unconditional peace talks". In the same spirit, we wish to emphasise the utmost importance we attach to agreeing to a time frame and a procedure for the continuation of peace talks, including the "fundamental political issues underlying the ethnic conflict". (See your letter of 16th March 1995).

With best wishes,
Yours Sincerely,

Chandrika Bandaranaike Kumaratunga

Though Kumaratunga's letter contained assertions of government supremacy and sarcastic innuendo, there were also elements of compromise. Of the four issues we raised, the government was prepared to concede to two matters. i.e. lifting the ban on fuel and fishing. Nevertheless we knew that these were reluctant decisions taken under the constraints of a deadline. We wanted to ensure that these decisions be implemented without delay. Fifty years of bitter historical experience had taught us about how Sinhala governments betrayed their pledges and agreements. Subsequently, we did not rush to withdraw our deadline simply on the basis of Chandrika's promises. Rather, we decided to extend the deadline for another three weeks to facilitate a time frame for the implementation of the decisions.

It was the first time President Kumaratunga admitted that the goods on which the embargo had been lifted were not reaching the Tamil people due 'to administrative and other impediments'. Her solution was to open an additional checkpoint. This new checkpoint also became an additional obstacle blocking the flow of lifted goods to the North.

Mr. Pirabakaran, in his reply, clarified Chandrika's misconception by arguing that the LTTE as a party in conflict reserved the right to set a deadline for the termination of peace talks if 'we are of the opinion that the negotiations have reached a stalemate with out producing any constructive results'. He also criticised Chandrika's conception of the LTTE as an armed group. Her perception 'was predicated on a mistaken conception', he charged. The LTTE was a national liberation movement, Mr. Pirabakaran declared, "deeply embedded with our people, articulating the wishes and aspirations of the Tamil nation". We publish below the full text of his letter.

LTTE Headquarters
Jaffna
28th March 1995

Hon. Chandrika Bandaranaike Kumaratunga
President of Sri Lanka
Presidential Secretariat
Colombo.

Dear President,

Thank you very much for your letter dated 24th March 1995. We have given careful and serious consideration to the contents of your communication in which we find positive elements of reconciliation to certain issues we raised. On that basis, we have decided to extend our deadline to 19th April 1995. This space of time will help to facilitate the speedy implementation of your decisions.

In your letter you have raised objections to the fixing of deadlines which you call 'ultimatum'. This is unavoidable since we have our own compulsions to ensure that the peace process should be a productive exercise that promotes the interests of our people. Furthermore, as a party to conflict involved in the negotiating process we reserve the right to set a deadline to terminate the peace process if we are of the opinion that the negotiations have reached a stalemate without producing any constructive results. We were compelled to set a deadline since the negotiating process reached an impasse without achieving any substantial results on certain urgent issues that seriously affected the conditions of our people. Now that you have made a favourable response to some of the issues we have raised, we have decided to extend our deadline for three weeks in the hope that you will implement your decisions and that the peace process could be advanced in a positive direction.

We are pleased to note that you have arrived at positive decisions with regard to lifting of the economic embargo, including fuel, and the removal of the restrictions on fishing. While we welcome your positive decisions on the above stated issues, we should insist that urgent and immediate action should be taken to implement these decisions without delay. I need not emphasise that decisions, pledges and promises have little or no relevance until and unless they are put into concrete practical implementation. It is to ensure that the implementation process should proceed without delay, we have set a deadline. I hope you will understand our apprehensions on this matter. In this context, we wish to point out that one of your earlier decisions, i.e. relaxation of the embargo on certain items, has not been properly implemented because of the obstructions caused by the military.

You have suggested that implementation of your decisions require mutual discussion with regard to some practical details.

We welcome your proposal and suggest an early date - 1ˢᵗ April 1995 - for such a dialogue.

We are disappointed to note that some of the other crucial issues we have raised are not addressed to our satisfaction in your latest communication. You are fully aware that an opening of a passage to Jaffna is of critical importance to our people. We have been insisting that the removal of the Pooneryn army camp would facilitate the free and unhindered movement of our people along Sangupitty causeway. Your response to this issue is negative in the sense that you have only reiterated your government's old position of shifting the front defence lines of the camp to 600 metres. On the question of the freedom of mobility of our armed cadres in the Eastern Province, your government has not so far made any conciliatory decisions. You will appreciate that the resolution of these issues is of crucial importance for the stabilisation of the conditions of peace, for the restoration of normalcy and for the promotion of peace negotiations. Therefore, we suggest that your forthcoming delegation is empowered to discuss these crucial matters.

In your letter you have listed a series of actions as concessions or rather privileges accorded to the LTTE by your Government to build up trust and confidence. According to you such actions included the initiation of peace talks without demanding the laying down of arms, declaration of cessation of hostilities, visiting of the Government peace delegation to Jaffna etc. It is wrong on your part to assume such actions constitute special privileges accorded to the LTTE, but rather, they should be viewed as necessary conditions to undertake a peace initiative. Your perception of the LTTE as an armed group is predicated on a mistaken conception. We are a national liberation movement deeply embedded with our people, articulating the wishes and aspirations of the Tamil nation. Having opted for unconditional peace negotiations with the LTTE in the implicit recognition of its predominate role, it is improper to designate the pre-requisites of the peace process as privileges accorded to the negotiating party.

Finally, I wish to state that the speedy implementation of your positive decisions and the earlier resolution of other important issues will certainly help to promote the peace talks that include political negotiations on the ethnic conflict.

With kind regards.
Yours Sincerely.

(V.Pirabakaran)
Leader
Liberation Tigers of Tamil Eelam

The Fourth Round of Talks

The fourth round of talks did not take place on the 1st of April 1995 as proposed by the LTTE leader. Chandrika was not keen to resume discussions on an early date to resolve the issues raised by the LTTE, but rather she deliberately delayed the process of direct talks. This delaying tactic was adopted to postpone the implementation of her 'positive decisions' and to offset the deadline stipulated by the LTTE. In a brief letter addressed to Mr. Pirabakaran, President Kumaratunga suggested 8th-10th April as suitable days for the fourth round of talks. She alleged that the LTTE had been campaigning that her government engaged in peace talks to obtain aid from the Aid Group meeting and to use it for military purposes. The context of the letter was aimed at defusing the Tiger's argument. She pointed out that a significant part of the Aid would be allocated to the 'reconstruction and development' of the Northeast devastated by war. The LTTE's campaign was based on hard facts that the Kumaratunga government had secretly undertaken a massive project of modernising the armed forces, assigning huge funds for defence, in preparation for an all out invasion of the North. It was only later that the international governments of the Aid Consortium realised how the Kumaratunga government wasted colossal amounts of funds both from internal resources and from external aid, for a war which led to the monumental destruction of the Tamil homeland.

On the 1st of April 1995, Chandrika sent the following letter to the leader of the Tamil Tigers:

1st April 1995

Mr. V. Pirabhakaran,
Leader,
L.T.T.E.
Jaffna.

Dear Mr. Pirabhakaran,

Thank you for your letter dated 28th March 1995, which I saw on my return from India on 30th March 1995.

Our delegation could visit Jaffna on any of the following days - 8th, 9th, 10th April.

The discussions would appertain to matters mentioned in our letter of 24th March and your response dated 28th March (page 2, para 3).

Please inform us which of these dates would be suitable to you.

We note that the LTTE has repeatedly in its communiqués in the recent past mentioned that our government is making efforts to enter into the 4th round of talks with the LTTE to coincide with the Aid Group in Paris, in order to derive an advantage to obtain Aid for Sri Lanka.

You have also stated that the government is trying by devious means, to secure funding ostensibly for economic development and use it for military operations.

I wish to impress upon you that: -

(a) The sincerity of our commitment to the Peace Process requires no further demonstration either for the international community or the people of Sri Lanka.

(b) The granting of Aid by the donor countries has already been decided upon, and is independent of our dialogue with the LTTE.

(c) The modalities relating to the grant of Aid are such that funds allocated for one purpose can not be utilised for another purpose and the use of these funds is subject to stringent international supervision.

(d) A considerable part of the Aid would be assigned by our government to the reconstruction and development of the North and East Provinces, devastated by the war.

If, however, you entertain any doubt on this issue, I am willing to postpone the visit of our delegation to Jaffna until after the conclusion of the Paris Talks. However, I wish to emphasise that our delegation is in readiness to undertake their visit to Jaffna on any of the dates indicated above.
With kind regards.
Yours sincerely,

Chandrika Bandaranaike Kumaratunga

The government was very subtle and sophisticated in the art of propaganda. Already an effective campaign had been launched internationally that the Sri Lankan state, in its endeavour to promote peace, harmony and reconciliation, had removed various bans, restrictions and embargoes in the Northeast. The government propagated the view that although the conditions for the normalisation of civilian life were restored, the LTTE leadership was still not prepared to engage in a political dialogue to resolve the ethnic conflict. But it was the LTTE as well as the Tamil people in the Northeast who knew the brutal reality of the objective situation in the Tamil areas. Though the government periodically issued Gazette notifications, and Chandrika wrote letters to the LTTE leadership proclaiming the relaxation of the embargoes, the bans and restrictions persisted. Irrespective of the assurances given by the government ensuring the free flow of goods to the Northeast, the army and the Defence Ministry were determined to enforce the blockade. The LTTE was also equally determined to pursue their line of approach constantly reminding the government of its deadline with the warning that the peace process would be terminated if the issues raised by the LTTE were not addressed, resolved and decisions implemented. As the fourth round of talks approached, the LTTE wanted to set its own agenda for talks. Mr. Pirabakaran insisted that the talks would be specifically confined to discussions 'on the modalities of implementation of your positive decisions' and other important issues raised by the LTTE. He also reminded Chandrika of his extended deadline (19th April 1995) as the time frame allowed for the implementation of the government's decisions and for the resolution of other critical issues. In conclusion, the Tiger leader emphasised the restoration of normalcy, stabilisation of the conditions of peace before entering into the advance stage of political negotiations. Mr. Pirabakaran's letter stated:

LTTE Headquarters
Jaffna
6th April 1995

Hon. Chandrika Bandaranaike Kumaratunga
President of Sri Lanka
Presidential Secretariat
Colombo.

Dear President,

Thank you for your letter dated 1st April 1995, which we received on the 2nd April 1995 through the good offices of the ICRC delegation in Jaffna.

The Government peace delegation is welcome to Jaffna on the 10th April 1995. Please inform us of the names of the delegates who will be participating in the talks.

We wish to state that in the fourth round of negotiations our agenda will be specifically confined to discussions on the modalities of implementation of your positive decisions and also about the two crucial issues we raised in our letter dated 28th March 1995. Our agenda is consistent with your letter of 24th March 1995 in which you have stated that you have arrived at positive decisions on issues raised by us, i.e. lifting of the embargo on fuel and removing all restrictions on fishing. You have also suggested that a dialogue between us is essential for the effective implementation of your decisions. In my letter of 28th March 1995, I have emphasised the critical importance of opening a passage to Jaffna by removing the army camp at Pooneryn and the free *mobility of our armed cadres in the Eastern province. These issues, along with your decisions will constitute the topics for discussions. You will appreciate that we have extended our deadline from 28th March 1995 to 19th April 1995 to facilitate your government a space of time to ensure the implementation of your decisions and to resolve other issues that are vital for the consolidation of the conditions of peace and for the normalisation of civilian life in Tamil areas.*

You are fully aware for the last six months, ever since the negotiating process began, we have been emphasising the utmost importance of resolving the most urgent and immediate problems faced by the people. We have been consistently arguing that the resolution of these issues in the early stages of the dialogue would facilitate and promote discussions on fundamental issues underlying the national conflict. Since your Government has shown little or no interest in resolving these issues and dragged its feet, we were compelled to set a deadline since we felt that the peace talks were stalemated and failed to serve any meaningful purpose. As I have explained in my latest communication, we, as a negotiating party, reserve the right to set a deadline for the termination of the peace talks if we are of the opinion that the negotiations have become futile, non-productive and have failed to serve the interests of our people. Since you have made conciliatory gestures on certain issues, we have extended our deadline to 19th April, with the anticipation that you will take immediate steps to implement your decisions and resolve other outstanding issues without delay. Therefore, we insist that the fourth round of talks would appertain to these matters, i.e. working out modalities for implementing decisions made by you and resolving the two issues we raised. We hope that the process of implementation of your decisions and the solution of the other matters will take place before the 19th April 1995.

Furthermore, we wish to reiterate that the day to day problems of our people are of paramount importance and need immediate and urgent solutions without further delay and resolution of these problems should be a prelude to political discussions on basic issues underlying the ethnic conflict. Our position has been that the creation of the conditions of normalcy by removing all restrictions, bans, sanctions, blockades, and the stabilisation of the conditions of peace by working out an effective ceasefire are of utmost importance before proceeding to the advanced stage of dialogue on the fundamental political issues. Therefore, we are not favourably disposed to the suggestion of working out time frames and procedures for political discourse at this conjuncture.

With best wishes.

Yours sincerely.

(V.Pirabakaran)
Leader
Liberation Tigers of Tamil Eelam

On the morning of 10th April 1995, a six member government delegation consisting of Rt. Rev. Bishop Kenneth Fernando, the Anglican Bishop of Colombo, Dr. Jeyadeva Uyangoda, a university lecturer, Mr. Charles Abeysekara, the chairman of the Movement for Inter-Racial Justice and Equality (MIRJE), Mr. K. Balapatabendi, the Secretary to the President, Brigadier S. Pieris (Army) Captain P.A.S. Rajaratne (Navy) arrived in Jaffna for the fourth round of talks.

Opening the dialogue, Mr. Tamilselvan insisted the discussion should be specifically confined to the modalities of implementation of the positive decisions made by the government and two other crucial issues i.e. the opening of a land route to the mainland and the freedom of mobility of the Tiger guerrillas in the Eastern province. The relaxation of the embargo on essential items as periodically announced by the government had become a matter of ridicule since none of these items reached the affected people, Mr. Tamilselvan complained. Pointing out that no progress had been made on the critical issues raised by the LTTE for the last six months he said that the talks had reached an impasse. It was precisely for the reason the LTTE was compelled to set a deadline for the termination of the dialogue. Bishop Kenneth Fernando queried whether it was an ultimatum. Mr. Tamilselvan said that he preferred to use the category deadline to denote the time frame for the conclusion of the talks and for the termination of the truce. He warned that the LTTE had no choice but to discontinue from participating in the peace talks if the government failed to implement the declared decisions and resolve the other critical issues before the extended deadline of 19th March 1995.

The new delegates (Bishop Fernando, Dr. Uyangoda and Mr. Abeysekara), though trusted emissaries of the President, had no political authority to make decisions. They gave a patient hearing and promised to carry the message to Colombo. Mr. Balapatabendi, Brigadier Pieris and Captain Rajaratne returned to Colombo on the same day whereas the new delegates stayed till the following day to continue the discussions. Bishop Kenneth Fernando requested a meeting with Mr. Pirabakaran but the LTTE leader was not available in Jaffna on that day.

The fourth round of talks ended as usual without any concrete decisions being made on any pertinent issues. We knew that the government team would report to the President on the Jaffna deliberations and that she would respond by written communication.

Chandrika Repeats The Promises

On the 12th of April 1995 Chandrika Kumaratunga despatched a communication to Mr. Pirabakaran specifying the government's proposed actions and 'reactions' with regard to four key issues raised by the LTTE. Apart from eight items which had military significance all other goods, including diesel and petrol could be freely transported to the North, she assured. Further relaxation of the restrictions on fishing was also announced. The other issues, i.e. removal of Pooneryn camp to open a passage to the Northern mainland and the free mobility of the armed LTTE cadres in the East had military significance, she said. Therefore these matters would be addressed in accordance with the progress made in the political discussions. In conclusion, Chandrika expressed relief that 'actions taken or propose to take' on the four issues would be satisfactory to the LTTE. The President's letter to the LTTE leader read as follows:

12th April 1995

To Mr. Pirabhakaran
Leader,
LTTE.

Dear Mr. Pirabhakaran,

We have considered the issues that were referred to in your letter of 6th April 1995; these also formed the subject matter of the talks that were held between our delegations on the 10th and 11th April in Jaffna.

I was glad to be informed that Mr. Tamil Selvan had, in the course of his opening remarks, stated that the date referred to in your letter was not to be construed as an ultimatum but as an indication of a time frame within which decisions already arrived at were to be implemented.

I will now set out the four issues referred to and the actions we propose to take and/or our reactions. We are of the view that these issues vary fundamentally in character. Considerable progress has been made with regard to some of these issues and we now propose to take further positive decisions designed to ameliorate the living conditions of the people in the North. However, it is evident that other issues have military repercussions; these issues will therefore have to be addressed in the context of progress to be made with regard to political discussions leading to a negotiated end to the war.

1. The Embargo:

Only the following items will now remain in on the list of goods prohibited for transport to the north:

Arms/ammunition
Explosives/Pyrotechnics
Remote Control Devices
Binoculars

Telescopes
Compasses
Cloth material resembling army uniforms
Penlight batteries

All other goods can be freely transported to the North.

The announcement of this decision will be made on the 13th April and thereafter a gazette will be immediately issued containing the list of 8 items still on the embargo list.

We have looked into your statements that earlier decisions on the embargo have not been fully implemented; we note that the free flow of items removed from the embargo list has been hampered by some obstacles. We have already taken and will continue to take firm action to ensure that all such obstacles are speedily removed and that goods can be transported to the North without impediment. As part of these efforts, we will also set up at all check points in and around Vavuniya civilian committees to whom any complaints can be made and immediate redress obtained.

2. Restrictions on Fishing

The restrictions on fishing, which were relaxed considerably by me on an earlier occasion, will be removed, taking into consideration your suggestions made to our delegation, so that fishing can be carried on at any time with only the following exceptions:

i. From Devil's Point to Thalaimannar fishing will be permitted only up to 5 nautical miles from the shore.

ii. Fishing will not be permitted within an area 1 mile either side along the coast and 2 nautical miles seawards from all security forces camps on the coast.

iii. Fishing will not be permitted in all bays, harbours and estuaries along the coast. Any problems arising with regard to the effect of this exception in the east should be discussed, as agreed with you, at a local level.

In the seas from Thondamannar to Devil's Point and in the Jaffna lagoon, fishing will be continued as at present.

The restrictions that remain are the minimum consonant with current conditions. The restriction on fishing in the seas from Devil's Point to Thalaimannar will be reviewed in three months time within which period, the government will make all efforts to conclude arrangements to permit fishing within Sri Lanka's territorial waters.

In removing the embargo on goods for civilian use including diesel and petrol and in removing restrictions on fishing to the minimum we have taken those steps that are necessary to alleviate the difficulties facing people in the North and to bring back to a state of normalcy civilian life. We are both agreed that this should be our joint first objective. I hope that with these measures and their implementation, we are well on our way to its achievement.

I shall now go on to the two remaining matters.

3. Pooneryn Camp

You have asked for the removal of the Pooneryn camp on the purported ground that the Sengupidy road cannot be opened up for civilian use without this. We have withdrawn the camp perimeter 600 meters and have given an undertaking to place no checks on the road and to allow unobstructed use of the road by civilians. We shall implement this.

However, it is not possible for us to take decisions on the removal of the camp at this time. The camp has military significance and it is also our understanding that under the Cessation of Hostilities Agreement, the status quo should be maintained and that neither side should attempt to affect the other's military capability. Nevertheless, conscious that the peace and normality we are striving to achieve must ultimately mean the reduction of military presences, we will keep this question under constant review and revert to it in three months time or when political talks are under way, whichever is earlier.

4. The Movement of armed LTTE cadres in the East.

We believe that this is a matter that should be negotiated within the context of the Cessation of Hostilities agreement. We are ready to discuss this immediately with you, negotiate an annex to the COH Agreement to include this as well as any other matters that are mutually deemed necessary, and to implement fully the conditions of this agreement including the activation of the peace committees envisaged therein.

We believe that the action we have taken or propose to take on the four issues raised will be satisfactory to you and provide a firm basis for the continuation of peace talks until they reach a conclusion in the resolution of the ethnic conflict.

In this context we suggest that the next round of talks center on

i. *the negotiation of an annex to the COH agreement.*

ii. *the finalisation of residual matters such as the Joint Authority on Rehabilitation and Reconstruction so that work may be expedited and*

iii. *the shape of future negotiations.*

We propose that these talks resume on any days between the 5th and 10th of May 1995.

Yours sincerely

*Chandrika Bandaranaike Kumaratunga
President*

The LTTE leadership was not satisfied with Chandrika's response. The only positive element in her communication was the decision to remove the embargo on fuel. Though promises were given to remove the obstacles in the flow of goods, we were sceptical about its practical implementation. There were still restrictions on fishing. On the other issues, she expressed apprehensions of military repercussions. The Pooneryn camp would not be removed but the front defence lines could be readjusted. No decision was made on the question of the freedom of mobility of our guerrilla fighters except an assurance that the matter would be discussed within the context of the declaration of the truce. Though Kumaratunga's letter was couched in a constructive mode with positive assurances, in essence it was a clever exercise in duplicity. In terms of concrete action or rather practical implementation, none of her assurances materialised.

The economic embargo continued in its usual rigidity. Even as the deadline approached, fuel and other essential items could not pass the military barriers at Vavuniya. With the blessing of the Defence bureaucracy, the army enforced its own blockade. Chandrika's promises turned out to be futile voices in the wilderness.

The ban on fishing continued as usual. The navy roamed the Northeastern waters and fired at fishermen and at the Sea Tigers who ventured into the seas in accordance with the terms and conditions of the relaxation of restrictions. The navy acted on its own as the master of the territorial waters of the Tamil region paying scant regard to the agreement reached at the peace talks and the assurances given by the President.

The Eastern Province continued to be tense as the Sri Lankan armed forces and the police continued harassing and intimidating the Tamil Tigers and prevented their movement. There were several provocative incidents, skirmishes and clashes. An incident occurred at Mandur, Batticaloa in which a senior LTTE cadre was compelled to commit suicide as he was severely assaulted and humiliated by the police in public. There were incidents of arrests in which our guerrilla fighters were forced to disarm. There was confusion among our ranks, as we could not give proper guidelines. The situation could not be prolonged any longer. Under the guise of the ill-defined truce the army took the upper hand in trying to suppress the activities of the LTTE guerrillas units.

The crucial matter that worried Mr. Pirabakaran was the continued build up of the Sri Lankan military machine as a formidable force. The purchase of modern weapon systems, the large-scale recruitment and training programme, the expansion of the navy and airforce clearly indicated that the government of Kumaratunga was modernising and enlarging the armed forces. We were curious as to why the new government, which claimed to be seriously committed to peace and had ushered in a peace process, was keen in building up the war machine. Such a move violated the very spirit of the truce agreement that demanded that neither party should attempt to offset the military capability of the other.

In view of the above factors, the LTTE was thrown into the dilemma of making a difficult decision as to whether to terminate or continue to participate in the peace process. We knew that negative decision would impair the image of the movement internationally. But at the same time, a positive decision would plunge the movement into a futile, meaningless exercise with far reaching military consequences. Mr. Pirabakaran was convinced that the Kumaratunga government was not genuine and was buying time for a hidden military agenda. I suggested another extension of the deadline. Mr. Pirabakaran was not favourably disposed to the idea arguing that it would not serve any meaningful purpose other than endangering our position militarily. There was growing dissent among the LTTE fighters over the protracted peace talks that were producing no positive results. Our field commanders had already cautioned Mr. Pirabakaran of the falling rate of morale among the cadres. There was a general feeling among our fighters that the terms and conditions of the truce agreement favoured the Sri Lankan security forces. The truce did not bring genuine conditions of peace and normalcy but rather seriously constrained the activities of our fighting units. The hatred and mutual hostility among the parties in conflict persisted. With the absence of peace committees to supervise the ground situation the animosity was aggravated. Mr. Pirabakaran was worried about the deteriorating situation in the East where the very survival of the mobile guerrilla units was threatened. Being a strict disciplinarian who demanded absolute dedication to the cause from his fighters, the Tiger leader was concerned about the growing demoralisation and sense of frustration among the fighters, particularly from the East. The other factor that we had to take into consideration was the growing disillusionment of the Tamil population over the peace talks. The hopes, expectations and the euphoria that manifested among the civilian masses at the beginning had now completely disappeared to be replaced by frustration, resentment and hopelessness. Our people felt that the peace talks had failed to resolve any of their urgent problems. They knew that the Kumaratunga government was not acting in good faith and the talks were on the verge of collapse.

As the deadline approached, the LTTE leadership realised that there was absolutely no meaning in continuing with this futile exercise. Even on the last day of the deadline Chandrika's promises of positive action did not materialise. Finally a decision was made to discontinue our participation in the peace talks and the from the cessation of hostilities. Accordingly the following letter was despatched to President Kumaratunga on the 18th of April 1995.

LTTE Headquarters
Jaffna
18th April 1995

Hon. Chandrika Bandaranaike Kumaratunga
President of Sri Lanka
Presidential Secretariat
Colombo.

Dear President,

Thank you for your letter dated 12th April 1995.

Having given careful and serious consideration to the contents of your communication, we regret to state that your responses and reactions to the urgent issues we raised fall short of our expectations and therefore, are unsatisfactory.

After a great deal of persuasion and dialogue, which lasted for more than six months, we were able to elicit from you a positive decision with regard to the relaxation of the embargo on fuel and other items. Though a decision to this effect has been made earlier and intimated to us in your letter of 24th March 1995, we are disappointed to note that deliberate delays have been caused in the process of implementation with the aim to off-set our deadline.

In so far as the other issues are concerned your response are partial, elusive, non-committal and subjected to determination of further dialogue.

Apart from partial relaxation, the prohibition on large areas of fishing zones continues to operate, though you have pledged to remove all restrictions on fishing in your letter dated 14th March.

On the most crucial issues of opening a passage to Jaffna by removing the Pooneryn army camp and the mobility of our armed cadres in Eastern Province, your decisions are unacceptable to us since they have been subjected to review in future discussions.

The manner in which these critical issues have been side tracked demonstrates the fact that your Government is not acting in good faith to create genuine conditions of peace and normalcy but rather seeks to promote the interests of the military. Furthermore, we are convinced beyond doubt, that your Government is making every effort to strengthen and consolidate the military capability of the armed forces under the guise of the current cessation of hostilities, violating the very terms of the agreement that insists on the maintenance of the status quo.

Since the above mentioned issues are not resolved to our satisfaction within the time frame set out in our deadline of 19th April 1995, we are left with no choice other than to take a painful decision to discontinue our participation in the negotiating process and from the cessation of hostilities from the stipulated date as we have indicated to you earlier.

We regret this unfortunate situation.

Yours Sincerely.

(V.Pirabakaran)
Leader
Liberation Tigers of Tamil Eelam

The letter brought to a conclusion the ill-fated peace talks between the Sri Lanka government and the Liberation Tigers. On the day of the deadline, 19th April 1995, the armed hostilities between the parties in conflict resumed when Sea Tiger commandos attacked and sank two Sri Lankan naval vessels inside Trincomalee harbour. The incident marked the beginning of, what some military analysts call, Eelam War Three.

With the resumption of the armed hostilities the propaganda apparatus of the Sri Lankan state swung into swift action unleashing a vicious smear campaign against the LTTE. Portraying the Tamil Tigers as 'villains of peace' the government blamed the 'intransigent attitude' of the LTTE as the primary cause for the breakdown of the peace talks. The Tigers were also condemned for terminating the cessation of hostilities without giving an adequate warning as required by the terms of the truce. In this context the government deliberately suppressed the truth that the deadlines given by the LTTE provided for an extended period of three weeks to enable the implementation of decisions. The main thrust of the state's propaganda campaign was to convince the international community that the LTTE was not amenable to a negotiated political settlement and therefore the government had no alternative but to pursue an all-out war to crush the Tamil resistance. The government succeeded in the propaganda war, convincing the world community that the LTTE was responsible for the breakdown of the peace talks.

The media was inaccessible to the LTTE for it to be able to articulate its position on the ill-fated peace talks. Isolated in the Jaffna peninsula and in the jungles of Vanni, the Tigers were practically cut-off from the rest of the world. Since the collapse of the talks the government had disconnected all communications with Jaffna. Journalists, local as well as international, were barred from entering the Northern mainland controlled by the LTTE. The State controlled media in Colombo was essentially racist and biased. The Indian media was mercilessly hostile to the LTTE. The world media was detached and uninvolved with the Tamil conflict and published only the government's version. In this estranged scenario the LTTE could not put up an effective defence against the vicious and calculated campaign by the government.

Reflections On Failure Of Talks

The international community was not fully aware of the peculiar modality in which the peace talks were conducted. It was primarily negotiations conducted at the level of exchanging letters between the leaders of the parties in conflict. By promoting this level of talks via written communication, the government deliberately subverted the role and significance of direct talks. During the six month period of the negotiations there were only four rounds of direct talks, each lasting for only a few hours of a day or two. The span of time allocated for direct negotiations was extremely limited in terms of the complexity of issues discussed. The government, by deliberately postponing the rounds of talks, allowed wide gaps in the negotiations to occur at times when the LTTE required further discussion and clarifications on crucial issues. And, most importantly, President Kumaratunga refused to delegate senior politicians of calibre, experience and authority to deal with the issues at the negotiating table. Instead, she nominated low ranking bureaucrats and military personnel who could neither understand the density of the problems nor had the political authority to deal with issues. This devaluation of the delegation, in our view, was aimed at belittling the importance of direct engagement. Even during the last round of talks, when the peace process was on the verge of collapse, Kumaratunga despatched a clergyman who lacked political experience or authority to deal with crucial issues, as the head of delegation. This deliberate depreciation of direct talks clearly demonstrates the fact that the government was neither earnest nor serious about engaging the Tamil Tigers in a direct negotiating process. While de-limiting the scope of direct talks, the Kumaratunga government gave prominence to written communications, a mode by which crucial matters were discussed, debated and decisions made. In all, more than seventy letters were exchanged between the Government and the Liberation Tigers during the entire period of the peace talks. Most of these letters were written with authority by the leadership of the parties in conflict. Yet this method of written exchanges failed to clear misunderstanding, clarify misconceptions and create mutual trust. On the contrary, the letters contributed to the gradual build up of distrust and hostility and also helped to reinforce the mutually entrenched positions widening the gap between the protagonists. Written in an over-patronising and condescending tone, some of the government's letters displayed the arrogance of the state authority treating the opponent (the LTTE) as inferior. Implicit in these letters was a denial to the Tamil Tigers the equal status of a combatant in armed conflict in a national liberation war. This aspect was a major irritant, compelling the LTTE leadership to respond with bitterness and hostility. As I have indicated earlier, most of the letters signed by Chandrika and her uncle Ratwatte, were cleverly constructed propaganda material intended to placate a different audience -Sinhala electorate- rather than addressing the issues raised by the Tamil Tigers. The propagandist intent inherent in the letters made the written dialogue unproductive and sterile. In our view, the primacy given to written correspondence by the Kumaratunga Government as the main form of dialogue, depreciating direct negotiations, was one of the cardinal factors for the breakdown of the Jaffna peace talks.

From the outset, the Sri Lankan military establishment was opposed to the peace talks between the Government and the Liberation Tigers. The military hierarchy adopted a rigid and uncompromising attitude towards the issues raised by the LTTE and created conditions for the eventual collapse of the peace talks. The military was vehemently opposed to any relaxation of the economic blockade, labelling all essential items vital for the life and survival of the Tamil community as military materials. The Government's occasional announcements of lifting essential items turned out to be exercises in duplicity since the army personnel guarding Vavuniya borders were determined to block essential goods reaching the

Tamil people. Though this matter was the central issue in the spoken and written dialogue and the LTTE termed it of 'paramount importance', no action was taken to redress this grievance. President Kumaratunga was well aware of the gravity of the issue yet she conveniently ignored it. For her it was an issue of 'national security' where 'strategic concerns' of the military had a predominant role, whereas for our people it was a life and death issue, an issue that affected the very core of their existence. For six months, the LTTE made maximum effort in the peace forum to secure the removal of this injustice but the Kumaratunga regime was ruthlessly determined to pursue oppressive conditions, to placate the military establishment, which finally led to the breakdown of talks. Furthermore, the Sri Lankan security forces were not favourably disposed to the LTTE's proposal for a permanent cease-fire supervised by an international monitoring committee. Even the fragile truce agreed upon by both parties was constantly jeopardised by the violations of the Government forces. Fiercely opposed to the mobility of the Tiger guerrilla fighters in the Eastern districts, the Sri Lankan army created intolerable conditions for the LTTE and made the truce agreement inoperative in the East. The army was also vehemently opposed to the LTTE's request for the removal of the Pooneryn camp so as to open up a safe passage to the Northern mainland. Pooneryn army camp and the Elephant Pass military complex formed a chain around the neck of the Jaffna peninsula isolating the densely populated region from the rest of the island. Tamil civilians had to undertake a perilous journey across Kilaly lagoon where the navy roamed, day and night, and mercilessly massacred the civilians who dared to cross the lagoon. Our people desperately needed a safe passage free from military harassment. This was why the LTTE suggested the opening of the Sangupitty causeway by removing the army camp at Pooneryn. If the Government had really been committed to a peaceful settlement with the LTTE, the relocation of the army camp would not have been a major disadvantage. But the Government, under mounting pressure from the military, fiercely resisted the LTTE's proposal. (Yet, later, in 1996, following a major military debacle at Mullaitivu, the Kumaratunga Government withdrew the army camp at Pooneryn claiming that it was isolated and unsafe.) The uncompromising hard-line position of the military establishment and its hostile attitude towards the LTTE was, in our assessment, a significant causal factor for the failure of the peace effort.

The events that unfolded following the collapse of the peace talks confirmed what we suspected as the secret agenda behind the Jaffna peace talks. Soon after the break-down of talks the Kumaratunga Government suddenly unveiled a devolution package for the solution to the ethnic conflict. The Government's propaganda machinery glorified the political package as radical and revolutionary offering 'more than the Tamils ever dreamt'. The world community was impressed and gave its blessings to the proposals believing that the Kumaratunga Government had found the right solution to the most intractable ethnic conflict in Asia. Having released the set of proposals the Government advanced a theory that a war was necessary to crush the 'enemies of peace' so as to realise a permanent peace with the implementation of the political package. The Tamil Tigers had already been condemned as the 'villains of peace'. In the government's view, the failure of the peace talks had demonstrated beyond doubt that the LTTE was opposed to a negotiated political settlement and therefore a major obstacle to peace. In these circumstances, the government declared that it had no choice but to unleash an all out war to wipe out the Tamil Tigers to secure a lasting political settlement and permanent peace. Now the ground work had been done for a major war effort in the name of peace. The government encapsulated this grand war strategy in a three word slogan called 'war for peace'. It was a remarkable strategy. A devious war plan was legitimised and rationalised as a necessary means to a permanent peace. In the calculation of the government the devolution proposals would attract wider support from the Tamil masses and therefore the LTTE would be alienated and isolated from popular support when an all out war was launched. But the Tamils, well grounded in the history of Sinhala chauvinism, were not impressed by the government's assurances of a permanent political solution. What the Tamils certainly knew was that an all out war was descending on their heads with its disastrous consequences.

The Buddhist monks set fire to copies of Kumaratunga's constitutional proposal.

The international community endorsed Sri Lanka's war plan mistakenly, believing that an escalated war would beget peace. It was unfortunate that the international governments uncritically approved this notorious war strategy totally disregarding the monumental tragedy that the war would inflict on a nation of people who were already suffering immensely under state oppression. Having secured the support of the international community with assurances of financial aid for the war campaign, the Kumaratunga government was emboldened to launch a massive arms procurement programme. The commanders of the armed forces were given permission to buy any type of modern weapon systems they needed to wipe out the Tamil Tigers. A massive troop build up took place in the Palaly military complex. A formidable force of fifty thousand troops were assembled from all over the island. The invasion of Jaffna, or rather, the 'Liberation of Jaffna', in the jargon of the government, began. The hidden scheme of the Kumaratunga government began to unfold in its monstrous forms. The secret agenda underlying the Jaffna peace talks became transparent and assumed the reality of a brutal war against the Tamil nation.

When she assumed office as the Head of State Chandrika Kumaratunga had an immaculate image as the angel of peace. She was able to convince everyone that peace was her cardinal mission in politics. It was that image that shielded her from any serious criticism when the peace talks collapsed. It was that image that deluded everyone to believe that her peace making effort with the Tamil Tigers was sincere and genuine. But as the turbulent history of her regime unfolded, spreading the flames of a savage war in the Tamil homeland, causing cataclysmic tragedies, her image underwent a radical transformation in the minds of the Tamil people. It was the nature of the brutal war and its deadly consequences on the lives of the Tamil civilian population that effected this change. Catastrophic events, unprecedented in the political history of the Tamils, have occurred throughout Chandrika's reign of office. The Sinhala army marched into Jaffna and occupied the cultural capital of the

Tamil nation which led to an unspeakable historical tragedy: the uprooting of half a million Tamil people in a huge exodus reminiscent of biblical times. While the Tamils suffered extreme humiliation and hardships, the Kumaratunga regime celebrated the conquest of Jaffna with pageant and pomp invoking the ancient rituals of Sinhala royalty - an event that had deeply wounded the soul of the Tamil nation. For more than five years Chandrika's 'war for peace' continued unabated consuming her first term of office with the mass slaughter of Tamil civilians, massive destruction of Tamil property and huge displacement of the Tamil population. It was the cruel nature of the war directed against the Tamil civilian masses that unmasked her peace image. The war had revealed her true face as a hardline Sinhala nationalist who was prepared to plunge the country into a cauldron of violence to deny Tamil aspirations for freedom, dignity and justice. Our people are now convinced, beyond doubt, that the Jaffna talks were a well orchestrated conspiracy to defame the Tamil freedom movement and to secure international support for a major war against the Tamil nation. The Tamil people, who overwhelmingly supported Kumaratunga to assume power for the first term of office as President, rejected her for the second term expressing their deep disenchantment with her administration.

Over the last five years, since the Jaffna peace talks collapsed, the war has been bloody and savage. The LTTE combat formations that withdrew to the Northern mainland of Vanni re-organised on a grand scale and fiercely resisted the offensive operations of the Sri Lankan forces. The armed forces suffered humiliating debacles and thousands of Government troops perished in the battle fields of Vanni. Having re-conquered all the lost territories in the Vanni mainland last year, the Tamil freedom fighters over-ran the 'impenetrable' military complex at Elephant Pass and liberated several strategic regions of the Jaffna peninsula forcing the occupation army on the defensive. As a consequence of these spectacular military victories by the LTTE, President Kumaratunga's 'war for peace' strategy crumbled. Contrary to what Chandrika dreamt, the war did not bring peace, rather it brought more war: it brought death and destruction on an unprecedented scale; it brought calamitous economic disaster to the entire island. The international community, which gave unconditional support to Kumaratunga's policy of 'war for peace', has realised that it has bet on the wrong horse. Despite this disastrous policy behind her, Kumaratunga refuses to give up the military option. Her second term of office began with the mobilisation of the entire Sinhala nation on a war footing. Having placed the country in the iron grip of emergency laws and tight censorship and having allocated huge funds for the purchase of modern weapon systems, Kumaratunga is gearing up for the next phase of a destructive war.

As she mobilised the Sinhala nation for war, President Kumaratunga knew in her heart that the passionate yearning of a people for freedom cannot be crushed by military might. She knew that the Tamil armed resistance is invincible as long as the political aspirations of the Tamil people are not fulfilled. Furthermore, she is aware that her government has already alienated and antagonised the Tamil people by a senseless policy of war and repression. And most importantly, the Western governments who uncritically supported her 'war for peace' strategy, have now realised the futility of the project and are advising her to seek a negotiated political settlement. These factors prompted Kumaratunga to resurrect the constitutional reform proposals of October 1997 as a way out to find a solution to the ethnic conflict. These reform proposals were the end product of a diluted version of the 1995 original devolution package. In her desire to seek a passage in Parliament for the new constitution with a two-thirds majority, Kumaratunga entered into a constitutional dialogue with the Opposition, the United National Party. Prolonged discussions between the two major Sinhala chauvinist political parties subjected the reform proposals to further dilutions and transmutations. In the end what was submitted in Parliament amidst so much controversy was a set of proposals that negated the basic demands of the Tamil people.

The Tamil people have been demanding the recognition of their historical homeland, their national identity as a distinct people and their right to determine their political status and destiny. These are the national aspirations of the Tamil people. These demands form the very basis of the nationality question of the Tamil Eelam people. A political framework that fails to address these fundamental issues underlying the Tamil nationality question is unacceptable to the Tamil people. Kumaratunga's constitutional proposals failed in this respect.

The entire controversial exercise of this constitution making and devolving powers was said to be aiming at solving the ethnic conflict. But Kumaratunga's reform proposals failed to address any of the basic demands of the Tamil people. The new constitution constituted a negation, or rather an anti-thesis of the basic Tamil demands for national identity, a homeland and self-determination. Though some loosely conceptualised categories invoke an abstract illusion of quasi-federal features, the state is conceived of as essentially a unitary structure super-imposing a 'Sri Lankan identity' over and above the quest for national identity of the Tamil people. The proposed draft constitution does not recognise the Tamil homeland. Instead, it contains a dangerous proposal for referendum on the question of merger of the North and Eastern provinces that will certainly lead to a permanent bifurcation of the Tamil homeland. As the draft constitution seeks to undermine the historical specificity and territorial integrity of the Tamil region, it cannot provide a basis for a regional autonomous structure that would satisfy the national aspirations of the Tamils. In terms of the exercise of power between the central institutions and regions, there are severe limitations detrimental to Tamil interests. It is beyond the scope of this study to provide a detailed critique of the constitutional proposals. But it is suffice to say that the new Constitutional draft fails to deal with crucial issues that form the core of the Tamil national aspirations and therefore totally unacceptable to the Tamils.

The tragic paradox behind this exercise of constitution making is that it neither satisfied the Tamils - the aggrieved party for whom the constitution is supposed to offer a solution - nor the Sinhala majority, who should be magnanimous enough to share power with the oppressed people. Instead, the constitution evoked violent resurgence of Sinhala-Buddhist chauvinism to dangerous levels of an open rebellion that forced the Government to abandon the Constitutional project half way. It was a setback for Kumaratunga's political design. The Buddhist Maha Sangha and the Sinhala hard-liners misjudged Kumaratunga's real intentions assuming that she was offering too much to the Tamils. But in reality she was offering too little, compelling even the Tamil "moderate" political party (TULF), a loyal partner faithful to Chandrika, to reject the proposals. The new constitution was not aimed at resolving the ethnic conflict in the real sense. Under the façade of a southern consensus, both Chandrika and Ranil colluded in whittling down the substance of the reform proposals. Compelled to confront the Tamil electorate in the coming Parliamentary elections, Chandrika wanted to dupe the Tamils as well as the world community as if she were proposing a 'federal solution'. In reality, the new constitution offered only limited devolution to the Tamils, whereas it conferred on Chandrika unprecedented executive powers to run the country as an autocrat. The constitution proposed to create an interim administrative body for the Northeast for a specific timeframe until a referendum which would eventually dismember the Tamil homeland forever. In creating the interim administration, Kumaratunga's real objective was to promote her Tamil quisling groups and to placate the Tamils so that the LTTE would be politically isolated and marginalised. This strategy, she assumed, would help her in her war effort to crush the Tamil freedom movement. Unfortunately for her, the chauvinistic forces could not grasp her Machiavellian design. It backfired, provoking the Buddhist clergy into an open revolt against the state.

The revolt of the Sangha against the state is not a strange occurrence in contemporary Sri Lankan history. In fact it is history re-enacting itself. The revolt has occurred at different times at specific conjunctural situations when attempts have been made by those in power to change the political structure to satisfy the Tamil demands. Several pacts and accords went up in flames as the temples of Buddha revolted and the fury of the saffron robes challenged the authority of the state. The supreme spiritual authority of the Maha Sangha did not hesitate to veto the decisions of the political establishment when it came to the question of sharing power with the other major ethnic nationality: the Tamils. The mythical Buddhist concept of 'dhammadipa' forbids such political practices. Sri Lanka, according to this doctrine, belongs exclusively to the Sinhala Buddhists. That was the will of Buddha, proclaims this ludicrous belief system, whereby the Sinhala race should own and rule this sacred island to preserve the pristine purity of his teaching. The Maha Sangha and its Orders of organised clergy lives by this ideological myth; the myth of the supremacy of the Sinhala race and religion. The racist ideology that rooted from this mythical belief regarded the Tamils as 'infidels of a degraded race' who should not be treated equally with the 'chosen people'.

The Maha Sangha and its organised clergy constitute the most powerful institutionalised structure of the Sinhala-Buddhist racist ideology. As the ideological apparatus of Sinhala-Buddhist hegemony, the Sangha wields unlimited power. The political system is subordinated to this religious Order which functions as a form of neo-theocracy imposing its will on the affairs of state. The Sangha, as the divine guardian of the Sinhala race and religion, has always championed the cause of majoritarian absolutism; the tyrannical system of the rule of the majority that does not allow any from of accommodation for the rights and liberties of other ethnic formations: particularly the Tamils. Embedded in a closed system of ethno-religious dogmatism, the Buddhist monks regard the Tamil quest for national identity and homeland as intolerable heresy and any attempts to resolve these demands, as treason. In this scenario, where Sinhala Buddhist racism dictates the rules of politics, the Tamil national question has become more complicated and intractable.

The draft constitution contains entrenched clauses that accord paramount importance to Buddhist religion and place the Maha Sangha on the highest pedestal as the spiritual guardians of the state and society. This special privilege was given to Buddhism to appease the Buddhist clergy disregarding the religious sentiments of millions of other non Sinhala-Buddhists living in the island. Nevertheless, the predominant role given to Buddhism failed to placate the monks and Sinhala-Buddhist hard-liners. On the contrary, they were furious that some devolution was offered to the Tamils. The very fact that what was offered was a fragile package concerning peripheral matters and that it was rejected by the Tamils as inadequate was completely ignored. What was intolerable or objectionable to the Sinhala-Buddhist chauvinistic forces was the very principle of power sharing with the non Sinhala-Buddhists. This is the dangerous aspect of Sinhala-Buddhist racism. This racism is not prepared to tolerate any attempt at reforming the existing political order allowing for any division of state power between the centre and periphery or rather between the majority and the minority nations. Sinhala- Buddhist racism has been jealously guarding a hegemonic desire that absolute state power should be vested in the hands of the Sinhala majority. This is precisely the reason and logic behind the uprisings of the saffron robes whenever attempts were made to reform the political order to transfer powers from the all powerful majoritarian political authority to regional structures on ethnic or geographical basis. The revolt of the Sangha is therefore a manifestation of racism: pure and simple. This racism, over decades, has grown into a powerful, unmanageable monster. It has a primitive feudal mind-set buried in ancient myths and therefore opposed to any structural changes in polity or in society. If this racism is sustained and fostered and is allowed to exercise its veto power over political determinations, then there is no hope for a negotiated political settlement to the Tamil national question.

The international governments, who are genuinely concerned about restoring peace and ethnic harmony to the island, should not ignore the threat posed by Sinhala-Buddhist racism to the peace processes aimed at ethnic reconciliation. This racism, well entrenched and widely institutionalised in the religious and political structures of the Sinhala social formation, has been the real impediment for peace and for the negotiated resolution of the Tamil ethnic conflict. The tragic political history of the Tamils, that spans more than half a century, with instances of deceits, double crosses and treacherous betrayals, illustrates a salient truth that Sinhala-Buddhist racism has been the real culprit behind all ill-fated attempts at resolving the Tamil ethnic conflict. It is not the so-called 'Tamil terrorism' that stands in the way of a negotiated political settlement but Sinhala-Buddhist racism that remains the stumbling block for peace. What is characterised as 'Tamil terrorism' is a bogey created by Sinhala-Buddhist racist forces to demean and discredit the armed struggle of the Tamil people and to justify an unjust war against the Tamil nation. Those who have taken up arms as the last resort to defend their people against racist oppression and tyranny are not terrorists. The real terrorists are those who preach the satanic doctrine of pure race and pristine religion and call for war, violence and bloodbath against the Tamil people.

Under the façade of a new constitution, the Kumaratunga regime aims to bury the national aspirations of the Tamils: their aspirations for a homeland and national identity. The racism that is hidden in her political discourse is very subtle and sophisticated. It is hidden behind the grand eloquence of one nation, of one people bound together by one and the only identity: the Sri Lankan identity. The subtle and invisible chauvinism of Kumaratunga is hidden behind her pluralist political doctrine, whereas the racism of the Sangha is crude and transparent. It is expressed openly in violent demonstrations, protests, fasts and speeches. Though there are qualitative differences in the manifestation of anti-Tamil racism in the political and religious orders, it is on the question of war, on the war against the Tamils, on the 'war for peace' both the Sangha and the government stand together as a single voice of Sinhala-Buddhist racism. It is in this realm, the realm of war, the subtle and the crude converge in a conspiracy to subjugate the Tamil nation. Only when the international community realises that the war unleashed against the Tamil people is an objective manifestation of Sinhala-Buddhist racism, will it desist from supporting the war effort by the Sri Lanka goverment which is aimed at the genocidal destruction of the Tamil nation.